MW01245279

The Heavenly Worship Room

Dr. Raelynn Parkin

The Heavenly Worship Room
Copyright © 2018 by Dr. Raelynn Parkin

Library of Congress Control Number:	2017947290
ISBN-13: Paperback:	978-1-64045-695-2
PDF:	978-1-64045-696-9
ePub:	978-1-64045-697-6
Kindle:	978-1-64045-698-3

Printed in the United States of America

LitFire
PUBLISHING

LitFire LLC
1-800-511-9787
www.litfirepublishing.com
order@litfirepublishing.com

Table of Contents

Dedication

This book is lovingly dedicated first of all
To my Lord who never left me
To my husband who stood by my side
To my children who comforted my heart
To my family who believed in me
To all those who encouraged me,
Supported me, and loved me in dry times
To all the intercessors who prayed
For the room and for the work being done
To all those who co-labored with me in
Bringing forth the Vision of the Room,

To Eddie Smith who encouraged me in perfecting this
work and giving it voice!
To Luis Chandler for your belief and LitFire Publishing
for finding its audience!

To Deborah Gray and Cathy Cuebas in their careful,
loving edit of the book.

To Dwayne La Rive for his beautiful picture of The Glory of the Lord

To Jamacia Johnson for her cover artwork and the Vision of the
Heavenly Worship Room

To Gary McClathcy for bringing the Heavenly Worship Room alive
with Worship!

To all the worshippers who have shared their
gifts with me over the years
And to the hungry worshippers who never
gave up believing that there was more!
This book is for you!

Preface

A Revelation of the New Testament
Holy of Holies

In my prequel, "Unlocking Worship Entering his Presence," I briefly introduced lessons and revelations concerning worship, the role of the worshipper, and restoring the Glory to the priesthood and to the church. The Heavenly Worship Room was originally completed in December 2009, and resubmitted for its first publishing in December 2014. In this book, we will further explore these concepts while unveiling the role of the Holy of Holies in the New Testament church. It is my heart's cry to see the Glory of the Lord return to his church, not just accepting that "all we see is all there is." There is more, and until I see the full manifestation of Heaven on earth, I must personally pursue this Heavenly worship. In the writing of these books, my heart's desire is not only to find it for myself, but to also open this door to the Body of Christ, and to see "His Glory fill the earth."

Towards the end of the previous book, the Lord revealed to me that "when the pattern is right, the Glory will come." This resonated through me like a lightning bolt, and I realized that it was the Lord's intention to reveal this to his church, because the Glory must precede his return. He is not coming back for less than what he originally left. He is coming for its fruition, the harvest at the end of the age, and the full maturity of his bride in the revelation of who He is. This last generation shall see the fullness of all things, including the glory of the latter house that shall surpass all things previously recorded, including the glory witnessed in the Word of God.

Jesus said that we would do even greater things than he did while on the earth, and he intends to fulfill his personal word to the church before his return. But its evidence may come forth with a backdrop of the darkness that is filling the earth, as the light is most greatly seen against darkness, as in a photo shoot. His early church spread under great persecution when he first ascended into Heaven, and unfortunately in the current world stage, this may occur again, even in a greater dimension. This is no news to the current believer, and is the very urgency I feel in writing this sequel.

As in the days of Moses, the only covering and shelter for the people of God was the Glory, as manifested by day as a pillar of cloud, and by night as a pillar of fire. And when the Egyptians pursued the Israelites, the pillar of fire was their rear guard, and hid them from the enemy, standing between them and the enemy who could not even see them through the fire. I believe again the only covering for the people of God is the Glory of the Lord, and so we must come into that place of His Refuge which is our shelter, our protection, our peace in the midst of surrounding storms as recorded in Psalm 91.

It is not my intention to rewrite or add to the Scriptures in any way, but to bring to light further revelation as to who we are and what our purpose is in light of a prophetic generation who will see the Return of their King. I believe this revelation is the opening of a door that has been previously overlooked or not fully understood in our day. It is more applicable for the believer of today than any other time in history, and necessary for what is looming on the horizon. I believe God always prepares his people through the prophetic word and strategies in advance of tribulation that his people will be immovable and unafraid, able to withstand the fire and to not fall away. This book is for the hearing ear and the willing heart that is searching for more than what they currently see in the church. So let us begin our journey of discovery together…

Dr. Raelynn Parkin

Chapter 1

In My Father's House

¹ Do not let your hearts be troubled. Trust in God; trust also in me. ² In my Father's house are many rooms; if it were not so, I would have told you. I am going there to prepare a place for you. ³ And if I go and prepare a place for you, I will come back and take you to be with me that you also may be where I am.

John 14:1-3 NIV

³ And if I go and prepare a place for you, I will come again, and receive you unto myself; that where I am, there ye may be also.

John 14:3 KJV

The Vision Begins

We were coming into a new place, the previous occupants were "The Father's House." We were now coming to reside and continue in the work that they had begun there. But it was a new work. And I, as the worship leader, was given a room, a small room on the right side of the platform about the size of a walk in closet, identical to the storage closet flanking the left side of the platform. I was given full authority to do whatever I wanted with the room, and the vision began to unfold as to the plan the Lord had for the room.

It was the beginning of October 2004, and the hand of the Lord was heavy upon me for about three days. I began to receive the download of the plans the Lord had, plans that overwhelmed me and frightened me. It was too much for me, and I did not even have the first clue in how to do what the Lord had given me to do. But I had resolved in my heart to give the best that I had to offer, and I would step forward in full faith and confidence that He would direct my path and lead me in the way to accomplish it. He had given me a pattern, one I had not even been aware of until now. He assured me this is how he led both Moses and David in the plans he had given them.

Moses' Pattern

> [9] Make this tabernacle and all its furnishings exactly like the pattern I will show you.
>
> Exodus 25:9

> [40] See that you make them according to the pattern shown you on the mountain.
>
> Exodus 25:40

> [44] "Our forefathers had the tabernacle of the Testimony with them in the desert. It had been made as God directed Moses, according to the pattern he had seen.
>
> Acts 7:44

> [5] They serve at a sanctuary that is a copy and shadow of what is in heaven. This is why Moses was warned when he was about to build the tabernacle: "See to it that you make everything according to the pattern shown you on the mountain."
>
> Hebrews 8:5

David's Pattern

> [10] "Consider now, for the LORD has chosen you to build a temple as a sanctuary. Be strong and do the work." [11] Then David gave his son Solomon the plans for the portico of the temple, its buildings, its storerooms, its upper parts, its inner rooms and the place of atonement. [12] He gave him the plans of all that the Spirit had put in his mind for the courts of the temple of the LORD and all the surrounding rooms, for the treasuries of the temple of God and for the treasuries for the dedicated things. [13] He gave him instructions for the divisions of

the priests and Levites, and for all the work of serving in the temple of the LORD, as well as for all the articles to be used in its service. ¹⁸ and the weight of the refined gold for the altar of incense. He also gave him the plan for the chariot, that is, the cherubim of gold that spread their wings and shelter the ark of the covenant of the LORD. ¹⁹ "All this," David said, "I have in writing from the hand of the LORD upon me, and he gave me understanding in all the details of the plan." ²⁰ David also said to Solomon his son, "Be strong and courageous, and do the work. Do not be afraid or discouraged, for the LORD God, my God, is with you. He will not fail you or forsake you until all the work for the service of the temple of the Lord is finished.

1 Chronicles 28:10-13, 18-20

In the last chapter of my previous book, "Unlocking Worship Entering His Presence," the Lord had spoken something very profound and wonderful to me. He said, "When the pattern is right, the Glory will come!" In writing the last chapter, "The Glory Returns," it became apparent to me that inherent in the pattern was the Glory waiting to be revealed. There was glory in the blueprints of Heaven given to men of things to come, and some of them were even symbolic of things to come.

⁷ "This is what the LORD Almighty says: 'If you will walk in my ways and keep my requirements, then you will govern my house and have charge of my courts, and I will give you a place among these standing here. ⁸ Listen, O high priest Joshua and your associates seated before you, who are men symbolic of things to come: I am going to bring my servant, the Branch.' "

Zechariah 3:7-8

These men were symbolic of the one to come, the Branch, the Lord Jesus Himself. There was Glory in the things that Jesus said and did and he also left us a pattern for his newly birthed church. There was Glory in His Word as well, waiting to be discovered. This is later reflection upon what the Lord had given me. Initially, I was too overwhelmed to even pen what I had seen. The hand of the Lord is heavy upon me now to recount the revelation of what he had given me four years previously. He said that I would now write this account in His Presence.

The Heavenly Worship Room

He showed me this room, but not all of the pieces at first. It was an unfolding revelation, as I would complete one aspect then he would show me another. I did not have the full revelation until I was nearing its completion. It was to be called "The Heavenly Worship Room" and I did come to understand the purpose of the room. It was a teaching room and had many lessons inherent in its design. He said I was building the prototype and I did not understand what he meant by that, but I saw many of these rooms going up around the nation and many nations. It was a prophetic work and a prophetic word to those who had ears to hear and eyes to see and hearts to perceive and understand. And it was beautiful beyond anything I could possibly have imagined.

Three Tabernacles

Inherent in the design of this room were three tabernacles, the tabernacle of Moses, the tabernacle of David, and the New Testament tabernacle of Jesus Christ.

> [11] "In that day I will restore David's fallen tent. I will repair its broken places, restore its ruins, and build it as it used to be,
>
> Amos 9:11 NIV
>
> [11] In that day will I raise up the tabernacle of David that is fallen, and close up the breaches thereof; and I will raise up his ruins, and I will build it as in the days of old:
>
> Amos 9:11 KJV

Incidentally, I don't think it is a coincidence that 9-11 has come to represent a terrible day of events or an emergency call. When God restores his 9-11, it will be an awesome day for the church as his Glory will be restored in the latter house.

⁹ The glory of this latter house shall be greater than of the former, saith the LORD of hosts: and in this place will I give peace, saith the LORD of hosts.

Haggai 2:9 KJV

Solomon penned this next verse, having built the former house.

¹ Unless the LORD builds the house, its builders labor in vain. Unless the LORD watches over the city, the watchmen stand guard in vain.

Psalm 127:1

What was in this tabernacle of David, this fallen tent that God wanted to restore? I believe it is significant that the Lord repeatedly says that **"I will raise... I will build...I will restore...I will repair."** He also declared that **"the glory of the latter house shall be greater than of the former...in this place will I give peace..."** and **"Unless the Lord builds the house, its builders labor in vain."** The main responsibility of the building and the restoration was upon the Lord's shoulders, he just needed an available and willing servant to bring forth his plans. I believe the tabernacle of David focused on his ministry before the ark and the former and latter houses focused on the resulting Glory that took up residence above the Mercy Seat. But I will go into further explanation in a later chapter.

The Vision Unfolds

I will recount what I saw in full vision and then I will revisit each aspect of the room. What I started with was the worst room in the entire building. The room had water dripping on its south side, an awful paint job and a border we could not scrape off the walls. It had black plastic baseboards which we tore off. It also had a huge speaker extended into the room and hideous green carpet with a small stair that entered the platform through a door. There were moldy ceiling tiles and it was an odd shaped room about 16 feet long and 12 feet at its widest and 9 feet at its shallow end where the speaker was. But we were happy to receive this room and the Lord had big plans for this room.

The initial part of this vision was to prepare the walls by putting Venetian plaster on the walls to cover up the bad border and paint job. I definitely had help doing this since I had never done this before. The Lord then showed me the Glory (gold) and the Blood (crimson) on the walls. It was to be present on each layer of paint on the walls. I began with a pale gold layer and then put splotches of gold and crimson on the walls, looking a lot like autumn leaves. Some cringed as they saw what was going up on the walls. My husband also helped me, knowing what I had told him, but not sure how to make it happen, and surely feeling my pain. I had seen the glory dance on the walls, but only God could do that part. Then God led me to the gold paint that went on top of this layer that made the walls shine like the Taj Mahal (some said). We then accented the lines of the plaster with shades of white and differing colors of gold and bronze faux.

The doors and facings were finished with ivory cream and the base boards were painted a faux copper and bronze to finish off the room strong. We intended to change out the carpet to a soft copper color with padding underneath as it was an unpadded concrete floor. An 8 X 12 rug was also purchased to cover the center of the room. To cover up the speaker, I found a soft iridescent gold fabric and used a plastic PVC pipe and curved it around the top of the ceiling to drape around the speaker. To complete that end of the room, gold fabric hung at the corners with soft ivory iridescent fabric and gold sashes draped over the top.

I then saw a floor lamp with a cream lamp in the far corner opposite the speaker, and there was a squared off pole on the far end of which I covered with the ivory material as well as in the far corner. Across the top border of the room, I saw light. So I found some crackled rope lights (Christmas lights) and hung them around the ceiling of the room, and then covered them with the iridescent ivory material to soften the light and create a beautiful soft glow. I had also planned to attach two beautiful sconces to the wall behind the platform to bring a softer feel to the room.

When the lights were turned off except the floor lamp and the ceiling lights, the room danced in the Glory, the walls had a life of their own. The Lord had done what he had promised, the walls danced in the Glory, and there was Glory in this room. There was an atmosphere of

Heaven, and as you entered the room, it felt like you left an earthly place and stepped into a place in Heaven.

I saw a chair in the corner in front of the floor lamp with a marble topped pedestal beside it. I then saw a short sculpted pedestal of which I had planned to put a vase with flowers. I painted it a cream base with gold accents on the sculpted carvings and it would sit in front of the ivory covered pole. I did not see many chairs in this place maybe one or two other chairs, as it was a very small room.

I then saw fabric on the ceiling and had no idea how to do it. There was an air conditioning vent in the center with the ugly ceiling tiles surrounding it. The Lord took me to an antique place with one room that was exactly what He had in mind. It looked like a pleated skirt, with pleats of ivory fabric precisely laid out from the far corners neatly tucked under the air conditioning vent. The air conditioning vent was perfectly covered with this ivory fabric to finish it off. I then saw different levels of ivory fabric hanging lower, like that of a tent, with varying degrees of height, but where you could see the gentle pleats above. These lower hanging fabrics that I originally saw, were not added in time for the completion of the vision.

He then showed me various accessories to finish the room. I saw a candelabra with one light raised above four. I found two of them the exact same style in two different stores in two different states, one smaller than the other with ivory taper candles. I saw a golden bowl for the incense of the prayer of the saints and I saw two large golden pillows, both the Lord took me to find in antique stores. I intended to find a Golden pitcher, or at least one that I could paint gold, but did not find it before the room was finished. And then He showed me the teachings of the room. These were actual stations of worship. I will describe them as they looked and then go into greater detail their purpose in a later chapter.

Three Stations of Worship

The first station of worship I saw looked like a golden bird bath. It was located at the end of the room where the speaker was. I looked high and low for this very bird bath, Romanesque and simple. I found one with the base and the bath in two separate pieces.

I painted them gold and copper with a coating of polyurethane since it would hold water. This was the Golden laver (though made of brass in Moses' tabernacle) as represented in the tabernacle of Moses. Located next to it was a golden accented basket which housed anointing oil and booklets of scripture to read.

Above it I saw a beautiful ornate golden oval mirror, the second station of worship. The Lord took me to an antique shop where I had seen the fabric on the ceiling and I spent a fraction of the cost for the most beautiful mirror I had ever seen. I hung it directly above the golden laver with soft ivory material draped behind it and hanging down to the floor. We see this in the heart of David and of Moses, to seek His Face. This is the mirror of what Jesus said and what he did. This is the mirror of beholding the Son and being transformed from Glory to Glory into the same image of that which we are beholding, the very likeness of our King.

> *18 And we, who with unveiled faces all reflect the Lord's glory, are being transformed into his likeness with ever-increasing glory, which comes from the Lord, who is the Spirit.*
>
> *2 Corinthians 3:18 NIV*
>
> *18 But we all, with open face beholding as in a glass the glory of the Lord, are changed into the same image from glory to glory, even as by the Spirit of the Lord.*
>
> *2 Corinthians 3:18 KJV*

The third station was the final crossing of the threshold into the Holy of Holies. I saw a table with a plate that had the bread and a wine glass, the one I found had a golden base with a red goblet which represented the blood of Jesus. These were the three teachings of the worship room, to teach the worshipper how to enter into the Holy of Holies, into the inner sanctum with Him, and how to approach a Holy King in the Throne Room of Heaven.

Beside this final station, I saw a doorway. I squared off its dimensions with gold fabric and lined the outer edges with the same ivory material used in the room. Behind this doorway was the platform itself. In front of this doorway, I saw two golden pillars which had two large angel candleholders set a little bit from the wall. The candelabra and golden bowl were positioned in front of the angels. These prophetically represented the cherubim that covered the mercy seat and the worship angels in Heaven. The vision went on to include two white pillars that framed this doorway and above the doorway was a valance that jutted out two feet from the wall and was fashioned as a throne. Hanging on the sides of the valance and parted in front was soft ivory tulle that could be seen through but represented the veil that was rent in two and opened for us. The veil was slightly parted though one had to press through to come into this inner sanctum with Him, the very Throne Room of Heaven. And behind this ivory tulle, was to be a picture of the Lord with his arms opened for us inviting us in to meet with him. This picture was to be a canvass rolled up as a scroll with two rods holding it up from its north and south borders. This picture was commissioned but never hung on the wall, nor was the Throne Valance finished to its completion.

To complete the teaching and function of this room, there was to be a prophetic log that each worshipper would record the scriptures, the experiences, the worship, the encounter they experienced with the Lord. Also there would be recording equipment hidden away but accessible to the worshipper to record the prophetic sounds and melodies and songs of Heaven that came through these experiences. I believed there to be a portal of Heaven in this room and that there were angels present. This room was to be a place of transportation into the Holy of Holies, the Throne Room of Heaven, to be seated in Heavenly places with Christ Jesus. It was to be a room of preparation for the worshipping priesthood to minister directly unto the Lord, a place where the Glory would reside, and a place of unending worship to an audience of One, the Lord Himself. This was a place where true worship was birthed in spirit and in truth, outside of the limelight and the applause of onlookers, but celebrated in the secret place. And it was to be an intimate place where the Bride and the Bride Groom could meet and fellowship, a place where the Love song of the Bride would move the heart of her King, a place of romance and the Dance.

This is the fullness of the revelation that was given to me by the Spirit four years ago, and as you can imagine, the enemy was on the prowl to steal, kill, and destroy this vision, as in Revelation 12. I fully anointed everything in the room and was able to capture the vision with pictures. I also exercised the teachings of this worship room three times and there was such an exquisite atmosphere of worship and glory present in the room each time. The final time He told me to come on in and just worship. A prophetic intercessor came into the room after the vision was put up and she saw the room empty. The Lord showed her the book of Esther and He said that he was preparing me for my night with the King. Incidentally this was one year before the movie, "One Night with the King" came out and in the final embrace of the movie, the outer room looked exactly as I had envisioned this room with its pillars and soft ivory fabrics and candles, but most of all the romance of the King and his Bride. A prophet had come into the church and declared that there was a tabernacle in Houston. He did not know that 15 feet behind him it stood. Another prophet had come into the church in February and had a vision of Jesus standing with his arms opened but he was behind a parted veil, because one had to press in to go into that secret place, that inner sanctum of the Holy of Holies. The worship room was dismantled the Friday before Thanksgiving, awaiting the resurrection of Amos 9:11.

> [11] "In that day I will restore David's fallen tent. I will repair its broken places, restore its ruins, and build it as it used to be,
>
> *Amos 9:11 NIV*

The teachings of the Heavenly Worship Room were published in Chapter 7 "Entering the Holy of Holies" of "Unlocking Worship Entering His Presence" in June 2007 and the "Unlocking Worship Teaching Series" in February 2008. One final revelation about this room came three weeks prior to our first ministry trip to South Africa in November 2008. The Lord quickened me that we were currently in the Jewish festival season of the Feast of Tabernacles, (also Feast of Booths or Feast of Sukkot) from October 14th-22nd of 2008. He quickened me to go and see when the Feast of Tabernacles was in the year of 2004. The Feast of Tabernacles in 2004 was between September 30th and October 8th. It was during this time that I began to receive the revelation of the Heavenly Worship Room, which was a Feast of three tabernacles, the Mosaic, the Davidic, and the New Testament Tabernacle of Jesus Christ. Now let's explore the scripture behind this revelation and teaching.

Vision of the Heavenly Worship Room, artwork by Jamacia Johnson at jamaciajohnson.com

The Glory of The Lord
Dwayne LaRive

Facebook.com/LaRive Artworks

Original Construction of the Heavenly Worship Room

Original Construction of the Heavenly Worship Room

Return to the Heavenly Worship Room
August 11ᵗʰ 2017

Return to the Heavenly Worship Room
August 11ᵗʰ 2017

Chapter 2

Three Tabernacles

Israel's Restoration

11 *"In that day I will restore David's fallen tent. I will repair its broken places, restore its ruins, and build it as it used to be,*

Amos 9:11 NIV

11 *In that day will I raise up the tabernacle of David that is fallen, and close up the breaches thereof; and I will raise up his ruins, and I will build it as in the days of old:*

Amos 9:11 KJV

It is interesting to me to see that there is something God says He will rebuild, he will restore, that he will raise up. In all of the many wonders of the earth, the natural and majestic mountains and waterfalls, canyons and painted horizons which all testify to His Glory, there is yet one thing that He will build. Of all the creative works of man that have been erected, from the pyramids and monuments to the awe inspiring cathedrals, even the decaying works of art that speak of the Creator of the Universe, He says he will restore a fallen tent. And even among the ancient buildings of his own people, the Temple of Solomon, where His own Glory dwelled, the future Temples that were later built, the palaces of the Kings, the walls of Jerusalem, and all of the places Jesus lived, God says He will raise up the Tabernacle of David. God describes very carefully his remodeling plan to restore its ruins. Obviously there is greater significance in what God intends to rebuild than just its physical characteristics or splendor.

Inherent in both of these versions of Amos 9:11 is obviously the Tabernacle of David, **"...and build it as it used to be,"** but also the Tabernacle of Moses, **"...and I will rebuild it as in the days of old."** Both of these tabernacles point to their fulfillment in the New Testament

Tabernacle of Jesus Christ Himself. In the Strong's Concordance of the Bible, the word tabernacle, is 5521 **cukkah or sookkaw,** a feminine version of 5520 **soke,** meaning a hut or lair, booth, cottage, covert, pavilion, tabernacle, tent. This also refers to the original word for tabernacle which is 4908 **mishkan,** meaning a residence, a shepherd's hut, the lair of animals, the grave, also the Temple, dwelling place, habitation, tabernacle, tent. There is so much to think about in the context of this word tabernacle. One of the more interesting meanings was the word booth or Succoth, similar to the tent Moses and the Israelites lived in during their wilderness journeys. Another connotation is the lair of animals as well as the grave, which depicts the sacrifice of another, death or the covering of skin. This was definitely demonstrated through the sacrifice of the Lamb, the death of our Lord Jesus Christ, as well as the grave to provide a covering of flesh. I am also reminded of the Tent of Meeting where Moses met face to face with God. How unfathomable is it to imagine that the Creator of all left His Splendor to meet in person with a man in a tent made of animal skins, filling its entrance with His Glory!

> [10] *Whenever the people saw the pillar of cloud standing at the entrance to the tent, they all stood and worshipped, each at the entrance to his tent.* [11] *The LORD would speak to Moses face to face, as a man speaks with his friend. Then Moses would return to the camp, but his young aide Joshua son of Nun did not leave the tent.*
> *Exodus 33:10-12*

Moses was in the Tent of Meeting in a face to face encounter with the Glory at the entrance of the tent, and the Word of God records that all of the people worshipped at the entrance of their tents. Could it be that the people are not worshipping because the leaders are not meeting up close and personally with God in His Glory? **Selah** I am also reminded that the actual Hebrew word used in this verse is the feminine version of the word, which I believe points to the Bride of Christ.

> *16 Know ye not that ye are the temple of God, and that the Spirit of God dwelleth in you? 17 If any man defile*

the temple of God, him shall God destroy; for the temple
of God is holy, which temple ye are.

1 Corinthians 3:16-17 KJV

The most prevalent meaning of the word tabernacle is residence, habitation, dwelling place, cottage, even as majestic as a pavilion. It is not as important that it is another building or housing project, but what is being housed in this dwelling place and what takes place within its perimeter. This is what I believe God is interested in building.

> [13] *"It is written," he said to them, "'My house will be called a house of prayer, but you are making it a den of robbers.'"*
>
> *Matthew 21:13*

This is what Jesus came to do, after all he was a Master Carpenter, overseeing the Spiritual House of Prayer that he was building for His Father.

> [1] *Unless the LORD builds the house, its builders labor in vain. Unless the LORD watches over the city, the watchmen stand guard in vain.*
>
> *Psalm 127:1*

Of course we have come full circle, the Lord says that He is building His House, which takes the burden of its completion off our shoulders, yet requires us to show up for work. Let us explore what it is the Lord declares that He will build, so that our labor is not in vain.

The Tabernacle of Moses

As we have already established, Amos 9:11 in the King James Version, declares, ***"... and I will build it as in the days of old:"*** I believe this definitely refers to the first Tabernacle recorded in scripture, the Tabernacle of Moses, its original intent and design, as well as what was established within the tabernacle.

> [40] *See that you make them according to the pattern shown you on the mountain.*
>
> *Exodus 25:40*

⁴⁴ "Our forefathers had the tabernacle of the Testimony with them in the desert. It had been made as God directed Moses, according to the pattern he had seen.

Acts 7:44

⁵ They serve at a sanctuary that is a copy and shadow of what is in heaven. This is why Moses was warned when he was about to build the tabernacle: "See to it that you make everything according to the pattern shown you on the mountain."

Hebrews 8:5

What we see in these verses is that Moses saw the original, the blueprint, the pattern which is a copy and a shadow of what is in Heaven. He had a Heavenly design and was commanded to do precisely according to the pattern he was shown on the mountain. God was the original architect and he personally led Moses on a guided tour in the model home that was in Heaven. The very thread of this pattern and design was of Heavenly substance. I believe God knows what he is doing, and likes things the way He wants them according to His own personal tastes. More than that, I believe there is a reverential fear for what is housed in this Heavenly model home, this Sanctuary: the Holiness and the Glory of God. It is also a copy and a shadow of what is in Heaven and I believe what was to come, the fulfillment of the embodied Tabernacle, the Word made Flesh that dwelled among us.

¹⁴ The Word became flesh and made his dwelling among us. We have seen his glory, the glory of the One and Only, who came from the Father, full of grace and truth.

John 1:14

Moses carefully did everything according to the pattern he was shown, which paved the way for the Glory to take up residence and dwell in the Most Holy Place, the Holy of Holies. Even today, we can glean from Moses' careful adherence to God's instructions which ultimately manifested in the Glory of God residing among the people. The Glory is inherent in its design, if we want to see His Glory, we must follow the pattern. We don't have to come up with the newest program or reinvent the wheel, we just have to carefully adhere to the pattern He has already given us.

There are many significant aspects of the Mosaic tabernacle that have already been explored which demonstrate the fulfillment of prophecy in the Life and Death of Christ, and many worthy studies that reveal Jesus Christ to us, of which I pray this discussion sparks you to further study. There are a few aspects I believe are very relevant to what God is building that I want to highlight, which cannot be thoroughly exhausted.

Protocol of Heaven

We tend to get bogged down in all of the traditions and the rules and regulations of what was established in Moses' Tabernacle, but I believe there was purpose in its facilitation.

> *12 The fire on the altar must be kept burning; it must not go out. Every morning the priest is to add firewood and arrange the burnt offering on the fire and burn the fat of the fellowship offerings on it. 13 The fire must be kept burning on the altar continuously; it must not go out.*
>
> *Leviticus 6:12-13*

> *23 Moses and Aaron then went into the Tent of Meeting. When they came out, they blessed the people; and the glory of the LORD appeared to all the people. 24 Fire came out from the presence of the LORD and consumed the burnt offering and the fat portions on the altar. And when all the people saw it, they shouted for joy and fell facedown.*
>
> *Leviticus 6:23-24*

In these two passages it is important to see the mandate of the fire to be kept burning, and never allowed to go out. In Leviticus 9:24, I believe we see why the fire was commanded to be kept burning. The source of this fire came straight from the Presence of the Lord, its origin was Heaven.

I believe this fire, whose source was Heaven, is what consumed the sacrifice and made the sacrifice acceptable. This fire came from the altar that is in Heaven as described in Isaiah 6: 6-7 when Isaiah cried out in the Presence of the Lord, **"Woe to me for I am a man of unclean lips..."** The angel then took a live coal from Heaven's altar, touched Isaiah's mouth, and said, ***"See this has touched your lips; your guilt is taken away and your sin atoned for."***

Unauthorized Fire

The Death of Nadab and Abihu

[1] Aaron's sons Nadab and Abihu took their censers, put fire in them and added incense; and they offered unauthorized fire before the LORD, contrary to his command. [2] So fire came out from the presence of the LORD and consumed them, and they died before the LORD. [3] Moses then said to Aaron, "This is what the LORD spoke of when he said: " 'Among those who approach me I will show myself holy; in the sight of all the people I will be honored.' " Aaron remained silent.

Leviticus 10:1-3

In this passage, we see that two of Aaron's own priestly sons offered up unauthorized fire, or as the King James Version calls it "foreign fire," before the Lord. Death was required of them because they did not adhere to God's instruction, his protocol. I believe this speaks of the severity of offering anything up that is not of Heavenly origin. The substance of which it is made is tested through the fire. It is better to have the work of your hands and your ministry tested and tried through fire on this side of eternity, than to stand before the Lord Jesus and give an account of your life's work, and watch it go up in flames. At least now we have grace to begin again and build a lasting reward through a life's ministry that truly honors the Lord, and to hear the words, "Well done, thou good and faithful servant..."

[11] For no one can lay any foundation other than the one already laid, which is Jesus Christ. [12] If any man builds on this foundation using gold, silver, costly stones, wood, hay or straw, [13] his work will be shown for what it is, because the Day will bring it to light. It will be revealed

with fire, and the fire will test the quality of each man's
work.
1 Corinthians 3:11-13

Reverence and the Fear of the Lord must come back into the House of the Lord. God established this in the Mosaic tabernacle, and it is as important today as it was then. I believe when we approach God with our talents, with our works, with a casualness or with a level of familiarity, this does not truly honor and respect a Holy God. We give greater honor to earthly Kings, we prepare in our most exquisite dress, we know how to properly approach His Royal Highness and honor their earthly protocols. How much more for a Holy and Righteous King whose Kingdom is forever and whom we serve!

Establishing the Priesthood

> [19] *"Aaron and his sons are to wash their hands and feet with water from it.*[20] *Whenever they enter the Tent of Meeting, they shall wash with water so that they will not die. Also, when they approach the altar to minister by presenting an offering made to the LORD by fire,* [21] *they shall wash their hands and feet so that they will not die. This is to be a lasting ordinance for Aaron and his descendants for the generations to come."*
> *Exodus 30:19-21*

I believe this is a lasting ordinance before the Lord to all generations of the priesthood. God established the priesthood, and gave them specific attire to show them honor before the people. He also required them to come before him in a consecrated way, with the washing of water, in the Bronze (Golden) Laver of the Mosaic Tabernacle. This physical cleansing speaks of a spiritual cleansing and that those who serve the Lord must be clean before Him. We all sing about wanting to see His Glory, but we must also know that His Glory and His Holiness are inseparable aspects of His Nature. As we saw before with Aaron's sons who died in the Presence of a Holy God, we know that death is required of us, if we are to enter into the Inner Sanctum where His Glory dwells. Flesh always dies in the Presence of the Glory.

We even see this in the New Testament with the story of Ananias and Sapphira, (Acts 5:1-9) and what they offered before the Lord. I believe they offered up foreign fire to the Lord in the Presence of His Glory and His Holiness, which resulted in their death. It is God's Grace that He has not visited us yet in the manner he did then. We need to die to the things of the flesh now, that we may enter in to the place where His Glory dwells.

Ezekiel's Standard for the Priesthood

As we explore the mandates of the priesthood first established by Moses in the first Tabernacle, we must also review Ezekiel's correction of the priesthood. There was a separation even amongst the priesthood as to those who ministered to the people and those who were allowed to come near unto the Lord.

> [10] " 'The Levites who went far from me when Israel went astray and who wandered from me after their idols must bear the consequences of their sin. [11] They may serve in my sanctuary, having charge of the gates of the temple and serving in it; they may slaughter the burnt offerings and sacrifices for the people and stand before the people and serve them. [12] But because they served them in the presence of their idols and made the house of Israel fall into sin, therefore I have sworn with uplifted hand that they must bear the consequences of their sin, declares the Sovereign LORD. [13] They are not to come near to serve me as priests or come near any of my holy things or my most holy offerings; they must bear the shame of their detestable practices.[14] Yet I will put them in charge of the duties of the temple and all the work that is to be done in it.' "[15]"But the priests, who are Levites and descendants of Zadok and who faithfully carried out the duties of my sanctuary when the Israelites went astray from me, are to come near to minister before me; they are to stand before me to offer sacrifices of fat and blood, declares the Sovereign LORD. [16] They alone are to enter my sanctuary; they alone are to come near my table to minister before me and perform my service. [23] They are to

*teach my people the difference between the holy and the
common and show them how to distinguish between the
unclean and the clean.' " ²⁴ " 'In any dispute, the priests
are to serve as judges and decide it according to my
ordinances. They are to keep my laws and my decrees for
all my appointed feasts, and they are to keep my Sabbaths
holy.' "*

Ezekiel 44:10-16, 23-24

This is probably the most specific and relevant issue today with the modern priesthood or the leaders in the church. Many have conformed to the worldly pattern of performance and entertainment, the American Idol Mentality that has invaded the Church's gates welcomed by its leaders with open arms.

As we see here, the priests performed their duties in the presence of idols. Performance is idolatry and we have preferred the counterfeit to the Glory of God. These priests still had their duties in the Temple and still ministered to the people. But these priests were not allowed near to the Lord or to serve from the Lord's table. This priesthood has little authority, little anointing, and no Glory or manifested Presence of the Lord in their ministry.

This second priesthood, the sons of Zadok, did not enter into idolatry and were faithful in their service to the Lord. Verse 16 says, ***"They alone are to enter my sanctuary; they alone are to come near my table to minister before me and perform my service."*** These priests do not just minister to the people, they minister unto the Lord. They do not cave into pressure to conform and usually stand apart. They refuse to enter into mixture and are willing to lay down their lives to protect the purity of what has been entrusted to them. They have His Fragrance upon their lives, they have great authority, great anointing, and they manifest the Glory of God, because they are allowed to come near unto Him. If you have eyes to see and ears to hear, you know which priesthood many leaders are members of, because of the fruit and the Manifested Glory.

*²³ They are to teach my people the difference between the
holy and the common and show them how to distinguish
between the unclean and the clean. ²⁴ " 'In any dispute,*

31

> *the priests are to serve as judges and decide it according to my ordinances. They are to keep my laws and my decrees for all my appointed feasts, and they are to keep my Sabbaths holy.*
>
>

Ezekiel 44:23-24

The fruit of this pure stance before the Lord is that they are given the responsibility to teach the people what is common (foreign fire) and what is Holy, what is clean and what is unclean, because they know the difference! They are also given the right to judge according to the Lord's standards, because ***they are His Standard.***

A Royal Priesthood

> *⁹ But you are a chosen people, a royal priesthood, a holy nation, a people belonging to God, that you may declare the praises of him who called you out of darkness into his wonderful light.*
>
>

1 Peter 2:9

The fruition of what God established in the priesthood of Moses' Tabernacle finds its full expression here in our calling and in our purpose. We are a nation of priests, called Holy by God, chosen and set apart from all others, belonging to God. If we are the Body of Christ, then we are a Body of priests, a royal priesthood who displays the Glory of God, manifesting His Light into the darkness. The darker it gets, the more Glorious His Light is displayed, as a spotlight on a backdrop of darkness. It is time for the priesthood to come into the full destiny we have been called unto, and as we offer up Holy and living sacrifices before the Lord, the world will witness the demonstration of who He is through us!

Chapter 3

The Tabernacle of David

To understand the significance of what God wants to build, the Tabernacle of David, we can glean insight into the man whose name is attached to it. It is interesting that two of the meanings of the word Tabernacle, a shepherd's hut and a lair of animals, David was very familiar with, after all he was a shepherd, and was accustomed to living in a shelter made of animal skins. I believe out in the shepherd's field, David's worship legacy was birthed as well as his personal relationship with his God.

> *²² After removing Saul, he made David their king. He testified concerning him: 'I have found David son of Jesse a man after my own heart; he will do everything I want him to do.' ²³ "From this man's descendants God has brought to Israel the Savior Jesus, as he promised.*
>
> *Acts 13:22-23*

Only one man did God testify was after His own heart, and that was David. And from this beautiful heart, God's only begotten Son came into this dying world to save and redeem it back to its original state. What else can we see from the heart of David?

> *⁸ I love the house where you live, O LORD, the place where your glory dwells.*
>
> *Psalm 26:8*

⁴ One thing I ask of the LORD, this is what I seek: that I may dwell in the house of the LORD all the days of my life, to gaze upon the beauty of the LORD and to seek him in his temple.

Psalm 27:4

¹ The LORD is my shepherd; I shall not want. ² He maketh me to lie down in green pastures: he leadeth me beside the still waters. ³ He restoreth my soul: he leadeth me in the paths of righteousness for his name's sake. ⁴ Yea, though I walk through the valley of the shadow of death, I will fear no evil: for thou art with me; thy rod and thy staff they comfort me. ⁵ Thou preparest a table before me in the presence of mine enemies: thou anointest my head with oil; my cup runneth over. ⁶ Surely goodness and mercy shall follow me all the days of my life: and I will dwell in the house of the LORD forever.

Psalm 23:1-6 KJV

Such a beautiful expression of worship came from the life of David! In Psalm 27:4, we see David's greatest desire, **...that I may dwell in the house of the LORD all the days of my life, that I may gaze upon the beauty of the LORD, and to seek him in his Temple."** To look upon the Lord meant death, even in David's day, but his desire to seek the face of the Lord was greater than his own demise. Though David was not a perfect man, and had great sin in his life, his heart was turned toward God through repentance and constant dependence upon his Lord. God never repealed his testimony of David, even though he fell into sin, but recorded it for all future generations to remember. There is one more aspect of David's heart we want to explore.

⁷ David said to Solomon: "My son, I had it in my heart to build a house for the Name of the LORD my God.

1 Chronicles 22:7

² King David rose to his feet and said: "Listen to me, my brothers and my people. I had it in my heart to build a house as a place of rest for the ark of the covenant of the LORD, for the footstool of our God, and I made plans to build it.

1 Chronicles 28:2

*⁷ "My father David had it in his heart to build a temple
for the Name of the LORD, the God of Israel. ⁸ But the
LORD said to my father David, 'Because it was in your
heart to build a temple for my Name, you did well to have
this in your heart. ⁹ Nevertheless, you are not the one to
build the temple, but your son, who is your own flesh
and blood—he is the one who will build the temple for
my Name.'*

2 Chronicles 6:7-9

As we see in these verses, it was always David's intention to build a
house for his God, in fact in Psalm 23:6, he declared that he would dwell
in the house of the Lord forever. David's son, Solomon would actually
build the physical Temple, but his descendent Jesus Christ would build
a spiritual House of Prayer for his Father. In fact David provided all his
personal wealth of gold and silver and other precious stones and metals
that furnished the interior of the Temple. You could say that his heart
was refined as pure gold, and that is what lined the inside of the Temple
as well as its furnishings.

Prophet, Priest, and King

Much of what we know of David's life was prophetic and spoke
of the One to come through his loins, Jesus Christ. We also see that
he prophesied through his music and it brought forth a spiritual
manifestation.

*²³ Whenever the spirit from God came upon Saul, David
would take his harp and play. Then relief would come
to Saul; he would feel better, and the evil spirit would
leave him.*

1 Samuel 16:23

David's entire worship ministry was derived from his prophesy on
his instrument, the harp. In 1 Chronicles 25, we have a glimpse of the
worship ministry David established.

*¹ David, together with the commanders of the army, set
apart some of the sons of Asaph, Heman and Jeduthun*

for the ministry of prophesying, accompanied by harps, lyres and cymbals. Here is the list of the men who performed this service: ² From the sons of Asaph: Zaccur, Joseph, Nethaniah and Asarelah. The sons of Asaph were under the supervision of Asaph, who prophesied under the king's supervision. ³ As for Jeduthun, from his sons: Gedaliah, Zeri, Jeshaiah, Shimei, Hashabiah and Mattithiah, six in all, under the supervision of their father Jeduthun, who prophesied, using the harp in thanking and praising the LORD. ⁴ As for Heman, from his sons: Bukkiah, Mattaniah, Uzziel, Shubael and Jerimoth; Hananiah, Hanani, Eliathah, Giddalti and Romamti-Ezer; Joshbekashah, Mallothi, Hothir and Mahazioth. ⁵ All these were sons of Heman the king's seer. They were given him through the promises of God to exalt him. God gave Heman fourteen sons and three daughters. ⁶ All these men were under the supervision of their fathers for the music of the temple of the LORD, with cymbals, lyres and harps, for the ministry at the house of God. Asaph, Jeduthun and Heman were under the supervision of the king. ⁷ Along with their relatives—all of them trained and skilled in music for the LORD -they numbered 288. ⁸ Young and old alike, teacher as well as student, cast lots for their duties.

1 Chronicles 25:1-8

In verse 6, David set apart the fathers to train up their sons in prophesying with their instruments in the Lord's ministry. These fathers were of course under the supervision of King David. They were all equally skilled in their music and cast lots for their position in the House of the Lord. Their talents did not land them their position, they were all equal, both students and teachers alike. I believe it was their heart that chose them for this position, as I believe it should be today in the church.

David also descended from the tribe of Judah, (meaning thanks or praise) yet God considered him of the priestly order.

³⁵ I will raise up for myself a faithful priest, who will do according to what is in my heart and mind. I will firmly establish his house, and he will minister before my anointed one always.

1 Samuel 2:35

Many believe this to be Samuel the priest, and others believe this to be Zadok. I believe this speaks of David, when he declares that he will firmly establish his house, and minister before my anointed one always, who I believe is Jesus Christ. David wore the ephod of the priestly garments when they transported the ark to its resting place in the tabernacle.

> [13] *When those who were carrying the ark of the LORD had taken six steps, he sacrificed a bull and a fattened calf.* [14] *David, wearing a linen ephod, danced before the LORD with all his might,* [15] *while he and the entire house of Israel brought up the ark of the LORD with shouts and the sound of trumpets.*
>
> *2 Samuel 6:13-15*

> [27] *Now David was clothed in a robe of fine linen, as were all the Levites who were carrying the ark, and as were the singers, and Kenaniah, who was in charge of the singing of the choirs. David also wore a linen ephod.*
>
> *1 Chronicles 15:27*

The ephod was one of the designated garments given to the priesthood to wear. David incurred no penalty when he wore the priestly garment. Moses established the original priesthood from the tribe of Levi or the Levitical families. David was of the tribe of Judah as was Jesus Christ the Messiah. Another priesthood is beginning to emerge.

> [13] *He of whom these things are said belonged to a different tribe, and no one from that tribe has ever served at the altar.* [14] *For it is clear that our Lord descended from Judah, and in regard to that tribe Moses said nothing about priests.*
>
> *Hebrews 7:13-14*

We all know David as the beloved King of Israel, the one God had promised to establish his throne forever.

¹⁸ I will establish your royal throne, as I covenanted with David your father when I said, 'You shall never fail to have a man to rule over Israel.'

2 Chronicles 7:18

⁷ Of the increase of his government and peace there will be no end. He will reign on David's throne and over his kingdom, establishing and upholding it with justice and righteousness from that time on and forever. The zeal of the LORD Almighty will accomplish this.

Isaiah 9:7

The Tabernacle is built

The journey of the Ark to its resting place in the Tabernacle is chronicled in 2 Samuel 6 and 1 Chronicles 15. In 1 Chronicles 13, David decides to bring the Ark into Jerusalem on a shiny new cart.

⁶ David and all the Israelites with him went to Baalah of Judah (Kiriath Jearim) to bring up from there the ark of God the LORD, who is enthroned between the cherubim—the ark that is called by the Name. ⁷ They moved the ark of God from Abinadab's house on a new cart, with Uzzah and Ahio guiding it. ⁸ David and all the Israelites were celebrating with all their might before God, with songs and with harps, lyres, tambourines, cymbals and trumpets. ⁹ When they came to the threshing floor of Kidon, Uzzah reached out his hand to steady the ark, because the oxen stumbled. ¹⁰ The LORD's anger burned against Uzzah, and he struck him down because he had put his hand on the ark. So he died there before God. ¹¹ Then David was angry because the LORD's wrath had broken out against Uzzah, and to this day that place is called Perez Uzzah. ¹² David was afraid of God that day and asked, "How can I ever bring the ark of God to me?" ¹³ He did not take the ark to be with him in the City of David. Instead, he took it aside to the house of Obed-Edom the Gittite. ¹⁴ The ark of God remained with the family of Obed-Edom in

his house for three months, and the LORD blessed his household and everything he had.

1 Chronicles 13:6-14

David's heart was in the right place in bringing the Ark to a more desirable location. He describes the Ark in verse 1 as *"...the ark of God the LORD, who is enthroned between the cherubim—the ark that is called by the Name."* The magnitude of what is described here is not that this is just a piece of furniture, but that it actually represents the one in Heaven, who is enthroned between the cherubim upon the Throne. He discovers that there is a right way and a wrong way that ended in death. Uzzah reached out to steady the Ark with his arm, which was declared by God to be an irreverent act, resulting in his immediate death. This is prevalent in today's church culture, where man tries to steady the anointing with the arm of flesh. David, of course is angry because he did not understand God's response.

Out of fear, King David stations the Ark in the house of Obed-Edom for about three months. The Word of God records that ObedEdom was abundantly blessed during that short period of time, because of what was residing in his living room, the Ark of God. I probably would have gotten my pillow and blanket and slept in front of the Ark had it been in my living room! David, after seeing the blessing upon Obed-Edom's house decides to try again, but this time, he does his research.

¹ After David had constructed buildings for himself in the City of David, he prepared a place for the ark of God and pitched a tent for it. ² Then David said, "No one but the Levites may carry the ark of God, because the LORD chose them to carry the ark of the LORD and to minister before him forever." ³ David assembled all Israel in Jerusalem to bring up the ark of the LORD to the place he had prepared for it. ⁴ He called together the descendants of Aaron and the Levites: ¹¹ Then David summoned Zadok and Abiathar the priests, and Uriel, Asaiah, Joel, Shemaiah, Eliel and Amminadab the Levites. ¹² He said to them, "You are the heads of the Levitical families; you and your fellow Levites are to consecrate yourselves and bring up the ark of the LORD, the God of Israel, to the place I have prepared for it. ¹³ It was because you, the Levites, did not bring it up the first time that the LORD our God broke out in anger against us. We did not inquire of him about how to do it in the prescribed way." ¹⁴ So the priests and Levites consecrated themselves in order to bring up the ark of the LORD, the God of Israel. ¹⁵ And the Levites carried the ark of God with the poles on their shoulders, as Moses had commanded in accordance with the word of the LORD.

1 Chronicles 15:1-4, 11-15

The key to this passage is that David with a repentant heart discovered that there was protocol in transporting the Ark. Not only does David command the Levites to consecrate themselves, which is in accordance with the laws of Moses, but he discovers the reason for God's anger in verse 13, ***"We did not inquire of him about how to do it in the prescribed way."*** He also refers to Moses' original instruction in the transporting of the Ark in verse 15, ***"...as Moses had commanded in accordance with the word of the LORD."*** In verses 16-24, David describes the entourage and celebration of the Ark as it makes its way to the Tabernacle David had constructed for it.

¹⁶ David told the leaders of the Levites to appoint their brothers as singers to sing joyful songs, accompanied by musical instruments: lyres, harps and cymbals. ¹⁷ So the Levites appointed Heman son of Joel; from his brothers, Asaph son of Berekiah; and from their brothers the Merarites, Ethan son of Kushaiah; ¹⁸ and with them their brothers next in rank: Zechariah, Jaaziel, Shemiramoth, Jehiel, Unni, Eliab, Benaiah, Maaseiah, Mattithiah, Eliphelehu, Mikneiah, Obed-Edom and Jeiel, the gatekeepers. ¹⁹ The musicians Heman, Asaph and Ethan were to sound the bronze cymbals; ²⁰ Zechariah, Aziel, Shemiramoth, Jehiel, Unni, Eliab, Maaseiah and Benaiah were to play the lyres according to alamoth , ²¹ and Mattithiah, Eliphelehu, Mikneiah, ObedEdom, Jeiel and Azaziah were to play the harps, directing according to sheminith. ²² Kenaniah the head Levite was in charge of the singing; that was his responsibility because he was skillful at it. ²³ Berekiah and Elkanah were to be doorkeepers for the ark. ²⁴ Shebaniah, Joshaphat, Nethanel, Amasai, Zechariah, Benaiah and Eliezer the priests were to blow trumpets before the ark of God. Obed-Edom and Jehiah were also to be doorkeepers for the ark. ²⁵ So David and the elders of Israel and the commanders of units of a thousand went to bring up the ark of the covenant of the LORD from the house of Obed-Edom, with rejoicing. ²⁶ Because God had helped the Levites who were carrying the ark of the covenant of the LORD, seven bulls and seven rams were sacrificed. ²⁷ Now David was clothed in a robe of fine linen, as were all the Levites who were carrying the ark, and as were the singers, and Kenaniah, who was in charge of the singing of the choirs. David also wore a linen ephod. ²⁸ So all Israel brought up the ark of the covenant of the LORD with shouts, with the sounding of rams' horns and trumpets, and of cymbals, and the playing of lyres and harps.

1 Chronicles 15:16-24, 25-28

I was tempted to just paraphrase this section, but it is so glorious an excursion in the care and the celebration of the Ark and who it represents. In verse 26, David reports, ***"Because God had helped the Levites who were carrying the Ark of the Covenant of the LORD...,"*** reminding us that He still helps us in carrying His Glory and His Presence through the Anointing and His Holy Spirit. We see the emergence of a worshipping priesthood which ushers the Ark of Glory to its resting place in the Tabernacle of David.

¹ They brought the ark of God and set it inside the tent that David had pitched for it, and they presented burnt offerings and fellowship offerings before God.² After David had finished sacrificing the burnt offerings and fellowship offerings, he blessed the people in the name of the LORD. ³ Then he gave a loaf of bread, a cake of dates and a cake of raisins to each Israelite man and woman. ⁴ He appointed some of the Levites to minister before the ark of the LORD, to make petition, to give thanks, and to praise the LORD, the God of Israel: [5] Asaph was the chief, Zechariah second, Then Jeiel, Shemiramoth, Jehiel, Mattithiah, Eliab, Benaiah, Obed-Edom and Jeiel. They were to play the lyres and harps, Asaph was to sound the cymbals, [6] and Benaiah and Jahaziel the priests were to blow the trumpets regularly before the ark of the covenant of God. [37] David left Asaph and his associates before the ark of the covenant of the LORD to minister there regularly, according to each day's requirements [41] With them were Heman and Jeduthun and the rest of those chosen and designated by name to give thanks to the LORD, "for his love endures forever." [42]Heman and Jeduthun were responsible for the sounding of the trumpets and cymbals and for the playing of the other instruments for sacred song. The sons of Jeduthun were stationed at the gate.

1 Chronicles 16:1-6, 37, 41-42

Thus the Tabernacle of David was established, with such celebration and glorious worship. It is important to note that there was a departure in the ministry of this priesthood from the previous priesthood. In Moses' tabernacle, there was a separation between the Most Holy Place or the Holy of Holies and every other part of the Tabernacle. Only the High Priest was allowed to enter one day a year this glorious and spectacular place, with bells on the hem of his robe, should he die from the consequence of an unclean life in the Glory and the Presence of a Holy God.

In the Tabernacle of David, the priesthood ministered regularly before the Ark of Glory, with no separation and no consequence of death. This was a ministry of praise and worship before the Ark, with the prophecy of musical instrumentation as well as singing of the words of David and other prophetic psalmists. These prophetic priests ministered regularly in the Tabernacle of David before the Ark for 33 years, every year our Lord Jesus lived on the earth. I believe it is a form of intercession as well as a prophetic utterance.

There were two distinct aspects of the Tabernacle of David that I believe God wants to rebuild and reestablish in the earth. The first is the Glory of God, which resided over the mercy seat above the cover of the ark. The second is the worshipping priesthood who ministered day and night before the Ark of Glory, in the Glory and Presence of God. This priesthood was prepared in front of the Ark, prepared in the Glory of God for 33 years, not in front of the people as today's church climate depicts.

Israel's Restoration

> 11 *"In that day I will restore David's fallen tent. I will repair its broken places, restore its ruins, and build it as it used to be,*
> > *Amos 9:11 NIV*

> 11 *In that day will I raise up the tabernacle of David that is fallen, and close up the breaches thereof; and I will raise up his ruins, and I will build it as in the days of old:*
> > *Amos 9:11 KJV*

God specifically declares that He will restore David's fallen tent or raise up the tabernacle of David that is fallen. I believe God wants to restore this ministry and this Glory in the earth. He wants to repair its breeches, which I believe speaks of this place of intercession in which this priesthood stood before the Lord.

> 30 *And I sought for a man among them, that should make up the hedge, and stand in the gap before me for the land, that I should not destroy it: but I found none.*
> > *Ezekiel 2:30 KJV*

The Lord wants to restore this place before him, this place also mentioned in Ezekiel 44:15-16, about the sons of Zadok who were allowed to come near to him, and allowed to minister from the Lord's table. God is calling back these prophetic musicians to again take their place before Him in His Glory and minister unto Him. These worshipping priests will again be consecrated unto this service and they will minister to the audience of the One and Only, not just in front of the people, but in the secret place, the Holy of Holies. They will have a fragrance of the Lord upon their lives, they will die to the flesh and things of the world, that they may enter this Holy place. They will be a priesthood prepared in the Glory, and they will radiate the Glory of God in their worship, their ministry, and I believe with unveiled faces, the Glory will radiate upon their countenance. When this priesthood takes their place before the Lord in the Glory, there will be an unprecedented result.

> [9] *The glory of this latter house shall be greater than of the former, saith the LORD of hosts: and in this place will I give peace, saith the LORD of hosts.*
>
> *Haggai 2:9*

The Lord declares that the glory of the latter house shall be greater than of the former house which refers to Solomon's Temple. By the time the Temple was finished, this glorious priesthood had been prepared in the Glory and worshipping in the Glory for 33 years. Let us see the result of this.

> [1] *When Solomon finished praying, fire came down from heaven and consumed the burnt offering and the sacrifices, and the glory of the LORD filled the temple.* [2] *The priests could not enter the temple of the LORD because the glory of the LORD filled it.* [3] *When all the Israelites saw the fire coming down and the glory of the LORD above the temple, they knelt on the pavement with their faces to the ground, and they worshiped and gave thanks to the LORD, saying, "He is good; his love endures forever."*
>
> *2 Chronicles 7:1-3*

This worshipping priesthood in unity of voice and instrumentation released the prophetic sound that ushered the Glory into his Residence above the mercy seat of the Ark in the Holy of Holies. This Glory was so magnificent, the priests could not enter or minister in the Temple. Have we seen this kind of Glory in the Church today? I believe we will see even greater Glory when we see this worshipping priesthood take up their position before the Lord in His Glory. He promises the Latter House shall be filled with a greater Glory, and we can take Him at his Word!

Chapter 4

The Tabernacle of Jesus Christ

14 The Word became flesh and made his dwelling among us. We have seen his glory, the glory of the One and Only, who came from the Father, full of grace and truth. 17 For the law was given through Moses; grace and truth came through Jesus Christ. 18 No one has ever seen God, but God the One and Only, who is at the Father's side, has made him known.

John1:14, 17-18

I believe God always intended to walk and dwell amongst his people, as he walked with Adam and Eve in the garden, he walked with Enoch, he conversed with Abraham, he spoke face to face with Moses, he comforted a lonely shepherd boy in David, and countless others throughout history. Since we could not ascend in our fallen state to a Holy God, he descended to our fallen stature as a flesh and blood man, that he would live among us, eat with us, drink with us, share our tears, and reveal Himself to us, up close and personally. He would actually lay down his life that he could bridge the gap our sin had caused and restore us back to his original intention, a people in communion and fellowship with the God of the Universe. I believe that was the joy set before Jesus as he endured the pain of the cross, a joyful family reunion with his Heavenly Father embracing his children. It was Jesus' greatest joy to reveal his Father to his disciples.

19 Jesus gave them this answer: "I tell you the truth, the Son can do nothing by himself; he can do only what he sees his Father doing, because whatever the Father does the Son also does.

John 5:19

⁶ Jesus answered, "I am the way and the truth and the life. No one comes to the Father except through me. ⁷ If you really knew me, you would know my Father as well. From now on, you do know him and have seen him." ⁸ Philip said, "Lord, show us the Father and that will be enough for us." ⁹ Jesus answered: "Don't you know me, Philip, even after I have been among you such a long time? Anyone who has seen me has seen the Father. How can you say, 'Show us the Father'?

John 14:6-9

This is one of the great mysteries, one that still boggles my mind. Jesus came to reveal his Father to the world, though his own did not recognize him. He was in such constant communion with his Father, I believe unbroken communion while he was on earth until the cross, that he could declare in such honesty that if you saw him, the Son, you had seen the Father. More so, that the Son did nothing of his own initiative, but *only* what he saw the Father do and what he saw in his Father's Presence. He did not even allow his own will to override the will of his Father as he faced his own excruciating death. Jesus also revealed the true purpose of his mission, he was not searching for true pray-ers, the Father was seeking true worshippers to worship him.

²³ But the hour cometh, and now is, when the true worshippers shall worship the Father in spirit and in truth: for the Father seeketh such to worship him.

John 4:23

Every Tabernacle ever constructed, as well as all the Temples erected had one purpose, and that was to bring forth true worshippers unto the Father. The regulations Moses was commanded to adhere to was to allow the Father to receive worship, if only through a veil, because of the sin of the people and the delayed appearance of the mediator who had not yet come. And yet His Glory was so magnificent, and dwelled among the people, if only seen by very few throughout history in the Most Holy Place.

I also believe it gave Jesus great joy to reveal Himself in His True form to a select few of his disciples, Peter, James, and John at the Mount of Transfiguration.

The Transfiguration

¹ After six days Jesus took with him Peter, James and John the brother of James, and led them up a high mountain by themselves. ² There he was transfigured before them. His face shone like the sun, and his clothes became as white as the light. ³ Just then there appeared before them Moses and Elijah, talking with Jesus. ⁴ Peter said to Jesus, "Lord, it is good for us to be here. If you wish, I will put up three shelters—one for you, one for Moses and one for Elijah." ⁵ While he was still speaking, a bright cloud enveloped them, and a voice from the cloud said, "This is my Son, whom I love; with him I am well pleased. Listen to him!" ⁶ When the disciples heard this, they fell facedown to the ground, terrified. ⁷ But Jesus came and touched them. "Get up," he said. "Don't be afraid." ⁸When they looked up, they saw no one except Jesus.

Matthew 17:1-8

Jesus was not just revealing Himself, but he had already told his disciples that if they had seen Him, they had seen the Father. His face shown like the sun and his clothes were white as light. What an awesome sight! And if that was not enough, they were then enveloped in a cloud, and out of the cloud, they heard the voice of the Father speak on behalf of the Son. I am sure they remembered the significance of the cloud from the stories about the wilderness days of Israel, and it was more than they could take! But notice the audacity of Peter in verse 4, he wants to build three shelters for them, one for Jesus, one for Moses, and one for Elias. Let's look at what the King James Version says.

⁴ Then answered Peter, and said unto Jesus, Lord, it is good for us to be here: if thou wilt, let us make here three tabernacles; one for thee, and one for Moses, and one for Elias.

Matthew 17:4

The word for tabernacles, found in the Strong's Concordance, is 4633 skene which is literally a tent or cloth hut, a habitation or tabernacle. It also refers to 4632 skeuos, literally meaning a vessel, implement, equipment, or apparatus. But figuratively, it is specifically about a ***wife*** as contributing to the usefulness of the husband. How amazing is that! Again we have a reference to the wife or the Bride of Christ! Could she actually be the embodied tabernacle that Jesus inhabits, one that contributes to his continued usefulness here on earth, the actual hands and feet of Jesus? ***Selah*** Reference to the three tabernacles here is significant, but I believe it was out of its time. First of all the Lord says that He will rebuild the tabernacle of David, so it is in His Timing. Secondly, Jesus had not yet fulfilled the most important part of the Tabernacle, the once for all sacrificial Lamb that would rend the veil between God and his people!

Jesus, the Tabernacle

> ²³ *"The virgin will be with child and will give birth to a son, and they will call him Immanuel"—which means, "God with us."*
>
> *Matthew 1:23*

Jesus was always intended to be the express image of the Father and his desire to be God with us, even before his appearance on earth. Let us explore some of the characteristics of Jesus as they relate to the Tabernacle, beginning with his function. Jesus was declared to be a High Priest in the order of Melchizedek.

> ¹⁷ *For it is declared: "You are a priest forever, in the order of Melchizedek."*
>
> *Hebrews 7:17*
>
> ⁴ *The LORD has sworn and will not change his mind: "You are a priest forever, in the order of Melchizedek."*
>
> *Psalm 110:4*
>
> ¹⁹ *We have this hope as an anchor for the soul, firm and secure. It enters the inner sanctuary behind the curtain,* ²⁰ *where Jesus, who went before us, has entered on our behalf. He has become a high priest forever, in the order of Melchizedek.*
>
> *Hebrews 6:19-20*

*4 No one takes this honor upon himself; he must be called
by God, just as Aaron was. 5 So Christ also did not take
upon himself the glory of becoming a high priest. But
God said to him, "You are my Son; today I have become
your Father." 6 And he says in another place, "You are
a priest forever, in the order of Melchizedek."7 During
the days of Jesus' life on earth, he offered up prayers and
petitions with loud cries and tears to the one who could
save him from death, and he was heard because of his
reverent submission. 8 Although he was a son, he learned
obedience from what he suffered 9 and, once made perfect,
he became the source of eternal salvation for all who obey
him 10 and was designated by God to be high priest in the
order of Melchizedek.*

Hebrews 5:4-10

In the Mosaic tabernacle, only the men from the tribe of Levi were
allowed to serve. Jesus as well as David descended from the tribe of Judah.

*13 He of whom these things are said belonged to a different
tribe, and no one from that tribe has ever served at the
altar. 14 For it is clear that our Lord descended from
Judah, and in regard to that tribe Moses said nothing
about priests.*

Hebrews 7:13-14

Let us explore the first time we are introduced to Melchizedek to
glean some important truths about Jesus' function.

*18 Then Melchizedek king of Salem brought out bread and
wine. He was priest of God Most High, 19 and he blessed
Abram, saying, "Blessed be Abram by God Most High,
Creator of heaven and earth.*

Genesis 14:18-19

Melchizedek the Priest

*1 This Melchizedek was king of Salem and priest of God
Most High. He met Abraham returning from the defeat
of the kings and blessed him, 2 and Abraham gave him*

a tenth of everything. First, his name means "king of righteousness"; then also, "king of Salem" means "king of peace." [3] Without father or mother, without genealogy, without beginning of days or end of life, like the Son of God he remains a priest forever.

Hebrews 7:1-3

It is important to know that the High Priest Melchizedek met with Abraham face to face and that he brought the bread and the wine to commune with Abraham. Jesus is the Manna from Heaven, his body was broken for us, and his blood the new wine, was poured out for us, representing the new covenant. This communion supper is similar to the supper that Jesus, our High Priest, offered his disciples in his last evening with them, and that we are commanded to continue to observe in his remembrance. This King's name meant Righteousness and Peace, and I believe all members of this order will exude this in their life. There was also an offering, the tithe given to this High Priest and an exchange of Blessing to Abraham. Remember that this original encounter predated Moses and the establishment of the priesthood through the tribe of Levi, the Levitical priesthood. (Hebrews 7:1-10)

I believe that David, of whom Jesus descended naturally, was not of the order of the Levitical priesthood, who received their job description from their bloodline and by natural inheritance. David was of a different order, a different priesthood. He was a prophetic picture of another type of priest, in the spiritual order of Melchizedek. Neither David nor his priesthood died when they ministered in front of the ark. The priests of the Levitical order up to that point were not allowed to go into the Holy of Holies. Only the High Priest could enter once a year, and he had better be clean or he would not survive the encounter. There was no veil that kept David or the priesthood he established out of the inner sanctum where the ark resided.

Just as Abraham met in person, face to face with Melchizedek and was blessed by him, so David was unafraid to meet the Lord in his sanctuary, to behold the beauty of the Lord, without the threat of the penalty of death. David established this ministry which prophesied this new order of priesthood, fulfilled in Jesus ultimate position, as High Priest in the order of Melchizedek. The priests of David's tabernacle ministered directly before the Ark of Glory, where there was no separation of veil, just as Melchizedek ministered directly to Abraham and Abraham submitted his offering directly to Melchizedek. The entire discussion of Jesus and Melchizedek is found in Hebrews 5 and 7, which merits further study.

Jesus Like Melchizedek

> [11] *If perfection could have been attained through the Levitical priesthood (for on the basis of it the law was given to the people), why was there still need for another priest to come—one in the order of Melchizedek, not in the order of Aaron?* [12] *For when there is a change of the priesthood, there must also be a change of the law.* [13] *He of whom these things are said belonged to a different tribe, and no one from that tribe has ever served at the altar.* [14] *For it is clear that our Lord descended from Judah, and in regard to that tribe Moses said nothing about priests.* [15] *And what we have said is even more clear if another priest like Melchizedek appears,* [16] *one who has become a priest not on the basis of a regulation as to his ancestry but on the basis of the power of an indestructible life.* [17] *For it is declared: "You are a priest forever, in the order of Melchizedek."* [18] *The former regulation is set aside because it was weak and useless* [19] *(for the law made nothing perfect), and a better hope is introduced, by which we draw near to God.* [20] *And it was not without an oath! Others became priests without any oath,* [21] *but he became a priest with an oath when God said to him: "The Lord has sworn and will not change his mind: 'You are a priest forever.'"* [22] *Because of this oath, Jesus has become the guarantee of a better covenant.* [28] *For the law appoints as high priests men who are weak; but the oath, which came after the law, appointed the Son, who has been made perfect forever.*
>
> Hebrews 7:11-22, 28

Because Jesus, the High Priest lives forever, his priesthood is permanent, and Jesus is forever interceding on our behalf with the Father. As High Priest he offered up his life once and for all, and there is no need for future sacrifices, as with the former priesthood. He lived a holy, pure and blameless life and is our example of a Holy and Righteous Priest.

The Mercy Seat

Let us now look at the Mercy Seat of the Ark as it relates to the New Testament and to Jesus Christ.

The Ark

> [10] *"Have them make a chest of acacia wood —two and a half cubits long, a cubit and a half wide, and a cubit and a half high.* [11] *Overlay it with pure gold, both inside and out, and make a gold molding around it.* [12] *Cast four gold rings for it and fasten them to its four feet, with two rings on one side and two rings on the other.* [13] *Then make poles of acacia wood and overlay them with gold.* [14] *Insert the poles into the rings on the sides of the chest to carry it.* [15] *The poles are to remain in the rings of this ark; they are not to be removed.* [16] *Then put in the ark the Testimony, which I will give you.*[17] *"Make an atonement cover of pure gold —two and a half cubits long and a cubit and a half wide.* [18] *And make two cherubim out of hammered gold at the ends of the cover.* [19] *Make one cherub on one end and the second cherub on the other; make the cherubim of one piece with the cover, at the two ends.* [20] *The cherubim are to have their wings spread upward, overshadowing the cover with them. The cherubim are to face each other, looking toward the cover.*[21] *Place the cover on top of the ark and put in the ark the Testimony, which I will give you.* [22] *There, above the cover between the two cherubim that are over the ark of the Testimony, I will meet with you and give you all my commands for the Israelites."*
> *Exodus 25:10-22*

This magnificent furnishing that represented, **"...the ark of God the LORD, who is enthroned between the cherubim—the ark that is called by the Name." (1 Chronicles 13:6)** had very specific instructions in its construction, from the gold overlaid inside and out, to the rings and the poles that were to remain with the ark for its transportation. In verses 17-22, I feel like we are literally transported to another dimension and that we are actually seeing what Heaven is like. The atonement cover which is also the Mercy Seat is placed over the ark with the Testimony within. In verse 22, the Mercy Seat is over the Ark of the Testimony which demonstrated that Mercy triumphs over judgment, and the New Covenant shall be seated above or covers over the Old Covenant of the Law.

The vision of the two cherubim placed at each end with wings spread upward, overshadowing the cover, is such a picture of what worship must be like in the Throne Room of Heaven. They are to face each other and to look toward the cover almost in anticipation of something. His promise is that He will meet with us, above the cover between these cherubim over the ark. I am reminded of the comforting Psalm of David. It is between the shadow of these wings, that the Glory of the Lord resided as referenced in both Moses tabernacle and the Temple of Solomon.

> *¹ He who dwells in the shelter of the Most High will rest in the shadow of the Almighty.*
>
> *Psalm 91:1*

Many believe that this picture and this archaic furnishing had its place only in ancient history with the exodus of Israel and that it is reserved for the pages of the Old Testament. I beg to differ. I believe we see the fulfillment of this in the New Testament as well in the life of Jesus, beginning with his birth.

> *⁸ And there were shepherds living out in the fields nearby, keeping watch over their flocks at night. ⁹ An angel of the Lord appeared to them, and the glory of the Lord shone around them, and they were terrified. ¹⁰ But the angel said to them, "Do not be afraid. I bring you good news of great joy that will be for all the people. ¹¹ Today in the town of David a Savior has been born to you; he is Christ the Lord. ¹² This will be a sign to you: You will find a baby wrapped in cloths and lying in a manger." ¹³ Suddenly a great company of the heavenly host appeared with the angel, praising God and saying, ¹⁴ "Glory to God in the highest, and on earth peace to men on whom his favor*

rests." [15] When the angels had left them and gone into heaven, the shepherds said to one another, "Let's go to Bethlehem and see this thing that has happened, which the Lord has told us about." So they hurried off and found Mary and Joseph, and the baby, who was lying in the manger.

Luke 2:8-16

The angels not only filled the sky in the announcement of Jesus' birth, but I believe they covered over the Lord Jesus as he lay in the manger, the first appearance of the Mercy Seat, made of hay. Consider that the shepherds were invited to this glorious display of angels rejoicing with wings spread looking to where the Lord Jesus lay.

[16] Let us therefore come boldly unto the throne of grace, that we may obtain mercy, and find grace to help in time of need.

Hebrews 4:16

The shepherds, who represented the common people, were allowed to come before the Mercy Seat and the One who sat upon it. Let's see the second fulfillment of the Ark of the Covenant.

[11] but Mary stood outside the tomb crying. As she wept, she bent over to look into the tomb [12] and saw two angels in white, seated where Jesus' body had been, one at the head and the other at the foot.

John 20:11-12

The two cherubim that were overlaid in gold upon the Mercy Seat of the Ark are represented here. I believe these two angels, one seated at the head and one seated at his feet, with arms spread upward looked toward the body of the Lord in anticipation of his Resurrection. It was as if they were covering the body of the Lord Jesus as in a Holy Dressing Room as he shed the perishable robes of fallen man and put on the imperishable robes of Righteousness and Eternity. The sound of rejoicing that must have been heard in Heaven as multitudes of angels covered the Throne Room and the angelic choir and orchestration that was released that day must have been deafening! The Lord Jesus perfectly fulfilled the Ark of the Covenant which was to meet, to dwell, to tabernacle, and to reside with his people.

Our final view of the mercy Seat demonstrated in the New Testament is found in these eternal glimpses of Heaven.

> *²⁰ which he exerted in Christ when he raised him from the dead and seated him at his right hand in the heavenly realms,*
>
> *Ephesians 1:20*

> *⁶⁹ But from now on, the Son of Man will be seated at the right hand of the mighty God."*
>
> *Luke 22:69*

> *¹ Since, then, you have been raised with Christ, set your hearts on things above, where Christ is seated at the right hand of God.*
>
> *Colossians 3:1*

This is the eternal Mercy Seat where Jesus is seated forever at the right hand of God. Let's take a brief look at his function and the function of this eternal priesthood.

> *⁹ After this I looked and there before me was a great multitude that no one could count, from every nation, tribe, people and language, standing before the throne and in front of the Lamb. They were wearing white robes and were holding palm branches in their hands. ¹⁰ And they cried out in a loud voice: "Salvation belongs to our God, who sits on the throne, and to the Lamb." ¹¹ All the angels were standing around the throne and around the elders and the four living creatures. They fell down on their faces before the throne and worshiped God, ¹² saying: "Amen! Praise and glory and wisdom and thanks and honor and power and strength be to our God for ever and ever. Amen!" ¹⁵ Therefore, they are before the throne of God and serve him day and night in his temple; and he who sits on the throne will spread his tent over them.*
>
> *Revelation 7:9-12, 15*

These are considered to be martyrs of the Great Tribulation, but I believe there are martyrs of every generation who lay down their lives to enter this Holy Place. They die to their flesh that they may serve the Lord in purity and Holiness. In verse 15 they are before the throne day and night in his temple, worshipping Him who sits upon the Throne. Jesus ministry was to reestablish the royal priesthood as seen in the following verses.

⁹ But you are a chosen people, a royal priesthood, a holy nation, a people belonging to God, that you may declare the praises of him who called you out of darkness into his wonderful light.

1 Peter 2:9

To him who loves us and has freed us from our sins by his blood, ⁶ and (Jesus) has made us to be a kingdom and priests to serve his God and Father—to him be glory and power for ever and ever! Amen. **Emphasis mine**.

Revelation 1:5b-6

The Key of David

We may not fully understand all that the Key of David unlocks and opens in this realm. But it is a great reassurance that it is in the Hands of our Savior, and that he knows what he is doing, opening the doors that can't be closed and closing doors that cannot be opened!

⁷ "To the angel of the church in Philadelphia write: These are the words of him who is holy and true, who holds the key of David. What he opens no one can shut, and what he shuts no one can open.

Revelation 3:7

A Door that is Closed

There is one door that remains closed mentioned in scripture. Let us visit this closed door in Ezekiel.

¹⁸ Then the glory of the LORD departed from over the threshold of the temple and stopped above the cherubim. ¹⁹ While I watched, the cherubim spread their wings and rose from the ground, and as they went, the wheels went with them. They stopped at the entrance to the east gate of the LORD's house, and the glory of the God of Israel was above them. ²⁰ These were the living creatures I had seen beneath the God of Israel by the Kebar River, and I realized that they were cherubim.

Ezekiel 10:18-20

²² Then the cherubim, with the wheels beside them, spread their wings, and the glory of the God of Israel was above them. ²³ The glory of the LORD went up from within the city and stopped above the mountain east of it.

Ezekiel 11:22-23

The Glory of the Lord passed through the east gate as it left the Temple, the City and the Mount of Olives, the mountain east of the city.

¹ Then the man brought me to the gate facing east, ² and I saw the glory of the God of Israel coming from the east. His voice was like the roar of rushing waters, and the land was radiant with his glory. ⁴ The glory of the LORD entered the temple through the gate facing east. ⁵ Then the Spirit lifted me up and brought me into the inner court, and the glory of the LORD filled the temple.

Ezekiel 43:1-2,4-5

¹ Then the man brought me back to the outer gate of the sanctuary, the one facing east, and it was shut. ² The LORD said to me, "This gate is to remain shut. It must not be opened; no one may enter through it. It is to remain shut because the LORD, the God of Israel, has entered through it. ³ The prince himself is the only one who may sit inside the gateway to eat in the presence of the LORD. He is to enter by way of the portico of the gateway and go out the same way." ⁴ Then the man brought me by way of the north gate to the front of the temple. I looked and saw the glory of the LORD filling the temple of the LORD, and I fell facedown.

Ezekiel 44:1-4

The Glory of the Lord left through the east gate and the Glory of the Lord is promised to return through this same east gate. But until then, this east gate remains shut, until the one with the Key reopens it and returns through it, promising the Return of the Glory again into this Temple. Incidentally, Ezekiel's Temple is one that has not been built, and I believe it is a spiritual Temple that was given to Ezekiel for the purpose of instructing the people about the regulations of this Temple. Possibly, it was given to illustrate the return of the Glory back into the earth through this east gate and the return of the king. He says that only the Prince is allowed to enter in and to sit here, the Prince of Peace. Look who will stand upon the Mount of Olives.

> [4] *On that day his feet will stand on the Mount of Olives, east of Jerusalem, and the Mount of Olives will be split in two from east to west, forming a great valley, with half of the mountain moving north and half moving south.*
> *Zechariah 14:4*

The last place the Glory touched the earth was on the Mount of Olives, and this is the exact place that the Lord will again touch the earth as he proceeds to unlock the East Gate and the Glory is ushered back into the Temple. The significance of the East Gate is that the tribe of Judah, the camp of the east, in Joshua's day led the Israelites. Judah or praise goes first before the mighty armies of the Lord and the Lion of Judah leads the way!

Jesus Holds the Key

I believe this key of David unlocks the worship that was birthed in David's Tabernacle. I believe it is also the establishing of the priesthood and the Kingdom together to serve His Father in Heaven. This key also unlocks the east gate in which the Glory of the Lord shall reenter the Temple and the earth. And this key is in the hands of our King and High Priest Jesus Christ who is establishing this royal priesthood and kingdom forever. Jesus Christ is the fulfillment of the Tabernacle, the fulfillment of the Ark of the Covenant and sits upon the Mercy Seat now in Heaven.

The Worship and the Glory that is before Him in this Holy of Holies Place shall be greater in this latter House of Glory than of the former house, according to Haggai 2:9. If that which was of the law was so Glorious, how much more will be the fulfillment and the fullness that we share as we approach the Consummation of the love between the Bride and her King? And what will the Bride look like? She will look like Him!

> [17] *Now the Lord is that Spirit: and where the Spirit of the Lord is, there is liberty.* [18] *But we all, with open face beholding as in a glass the glory of the Lord, are changed into the same image from glory to glory, even as by the Spirit of the Lord.*
>
> *2 Corinthians 3:17-18*

Chapter 5

The Feasts Revealed in Jesus

16 Therefore do not let anyone judge you by what you eat or drink, or with regard to a religious festival, a New Moon celebration or a Sabbath day. 17 These are a shadow of the things that were to come; the reality, however, is found in Christ.

Colossians 2:16-17

In our discussion of the revelation of Jesus in the tabernacles, we must also visit the Holy Feasts that God appointed for his people to observe, as they would also reveal the One to come, our Savior Jesus Christ.

Please understand that in the unveiling of the importance of these feasts, in no way do I intend to revert back from the time of Grace that is upon the Church to go back under the Law, nor do I subscribe to a substitution philosophy where the Church replaces or supersedes the "Apple of God's Eye," the Jewish people. The precious promises of God came through the Jewish heritage prophesied through the Jewish people, ultimately through Jesus Christ our Lord, and we as the Church are engrafted into that spiritual vine, that spiritual heritage. I believe both the Jewish people and the Church have their destinies yet to fulfill which will culminate in the One New Man, both Jewish and the Gentile Church of Jesus Christ coming together in salvation and in unity. I believe every Word of God is applicable to both the Jewish believer as well as to the Gentile believer and we can celebrate together all that God intended for us which was to dwell with him forever, and that all nations would come into salvation provided through the death of His Son, Jesus Christ. With that said, let us visit these feasts, as welcome observers and participants in the Glorious provision of our God.

> [1] *The LORD said to Moses,* [2] *"Speak to the Israelites and say to them: 'These are my appointed feasts, the appointed feasts of the LORD, which you are to proclaim as sacred assemblies.* [3] *There are six days when you may work, but the seventh day is a Sabbath of rest, a day of sacred assembly. You are not to do any work; wherever you live, it is a Sabbath to the LORD.'* [4] *These are the LORD's appointed feasts, the sacred assemblies you are to proclaim at their appointed times:"*
>
> *Leviticus 23:1- 4*

In Leviticus 23, the Lord establishes his appointed feasts for the people to observe as sacred assemblies at their appointed times. He first establishes the Sabbath Day (vs. 3) which is the seventh day of rest after six days of work in which they are also to proclaim a sacred assembly. In Leviticus 25:1-7, he established the Sabbath Year or the seventh year which commands a year of rest from the harvesting of the lands. He then established the Year of Jubilee in Leviticus 25:8-55, which is seven Sabbath years or 49 years, and is a year of rest on the 50th year. This is a year of redemption, cancellation of debts, liberation of the captives, lands returned to the original family owners, and a year of rest for God's people. Can we see how important the Sabbath Rest is to the Lord concerning his people? After all he commands us to labor to enter into His Rest.

> [10] *For he that is entered into his rest, he also hath ceased from his own works, as God did from his.* [11] *Let us labour therefore to enter into that rest, lest any man fall after the same example of unbelief.*
>
> *Hebrews 4:10-11*

It is also important to know that High holy days were declared as part of these feasts and were also called Sabbaths in observance of these feasts. They were also days of rest, where no work was to be performed and usually a sacred assembly was required. They did not always coincide with the traditional Sabbath, beginning at sunset of Friday evening and ending at sunset of Saturday evening, but signified the beginning and/or end of the Holy Feasts. When the scripture speaks of Sabbaths, they may be traditional Sabbaths, or they may be High Holy Days of Sabbath or rest in accordance with these Feasts.

These appointed feasts, which also coincide naturally with the seasons, begin with the Spring Feasts, typically from March to April, which are the Lord's Passover (vs. 5), the Feast of Unleavened Bread (vs. 6-8), and the Feast of Firstfruits (vs. 9-14). The summer feast from May to June is the Feast of Weeks or Pentecost, also known as Harvest (vs. 15-22). The fall feasts from September to October begin with the Feast of Trumpets, later called Rosh Hashanah or their New Year's Day (vs. 23-25), the Day of Atonement also called Yom Kippur (vs. 26-32), and the feast of Tabernacles also called the Feast of Booths (Sukkot) or the Feast of Ingathering(vs. 33-44).

It is important for us to understand that God does not expect us to go back under the law in strict adherence to these God appointed feasts. I believe He appointed the feasts as they would speak or prophesy the One who He was sending who would fulfill every aspect of these Holy Feasts. If we look carefully, not only do we see feasts that coincide with three seasons, spring, summer, and fall, but we see the feasts grouped into three days of the Church. The spring feasts coincide with the First Day (salvation), the summer feast corresponds with the Second day (Pentecost or the gifts of the Holy Spirit), and the fall feasts relate to the Third day or the Great Harvest of the Age (Hosea 6:1-2). I believe we can also see the ingredients of Revival through each one of these feasts. Let us briefly see how each one of these Holy Feasts correspond to our Savior Jesus Christ and His Church.

The Lord's Passover

In Exodus 12, the story of Passover and the regulations concerning this observance are given. As you remember from the Bible stories of your childhood, the Lord was about to send the destroyer angel through all of Egypt to kill all the firstborn males in the land as a judgment against the gods of Egypt and those who worshipped those false gods. God provided for his own people a way of escape by instructing them to kill a year-old male lamb without defect and to spread the blood on the doorposts of their house, so the destroyer would "pass over" their homes and not be allowed to enter to destroy their firstborn sons.

They were also instructed to be ready to leave and eat in haste, thus making bread without yeast which symbolized sin, as well as roast all of the parts of the Lamb to eat along with this unleavened bread and bitter herbs as part of this meal. Nothing was to be left of the lamb by the morning and there were to be no broken bones. It is interesting that God calls this Passover the first month, which denotes the beginning of their deliverance.

This feast of course prophesies the Sacrificial Lamb who shed his blood on our behalf, Jesus Christ. Jesus celebrated the Passover with his disciples.

The Lord's Supper

> [12] *And the first day of unleavened bread, when they killed the passover, his disciples said unto him, Where wilt thou that we go and prepare that thou mayest eat the passover?*
> *Mark 14:12*

He observed the Passover during the Lord's Supper and also introduced the New Covenant with the Bread (He was the Manna from Heaven, the Bread of Life) and the new Wine (His Blood was shed as the promise of a New Covenant). Jesus was crucified and in the grave before the end of Passover which was twilight of the next day. Some believe that Jesus was dead at the exact time as the time of Passover when all lambs were to be slaughtered and the blood applied to the doorposts of the Israelites. The people were commanded to not have anything left of the lamb for morning or burn its remains, and that none of the bones were to be broken as was demonstrated by Jesus' death. He was not left hanging on the tree but was already in the grave by the end of the Passover day, with no broken bones.

> [31] *Now it was the day of Preparation, and the next day was to be a special Sabbath. Because the Jews did not want the bodies left on the crosses during the Sabbath, they asked Pilate to have the legs broken and the bodies taken down.*
>
> *John 19:31*

Incidentally, during this Passover Week, this special Sabbath mentioned in the verse above, was also called the High Sabbath and was traditionally observed on a Wednesday, between the normal Sabbaths. The Passover lamb and our Passover Lamb, Jesus Christ, were both sacrificed on this day of Passover.

Jesus observed Passover with his disciples at the Lord's Supper at the beginning of the Passover and was also crucified by the twilight of the Passover day.

He was without defect, as professed by Pilate, "I find in him no fault at all (John 18:38). Jesus was once and for all the sacrificial lamb, in which the shedding of his blood allowed death to pass over those who accepted his sacrifice, and the beginning of new life to enter in as part of the New Covenant for the believer. He continues to extend this invitation even today!

> *20 Here I am! I stand at the door and knock. If anyone hears my voice and opens the door, I will come in and eat with him, and he with me.*
>
> *Revelation 3:20*

The Feast of Unleavened Bread

In Leviticus 23:6-8, after the completion of the Passover day, this feast begins at the twilight of the next day and lasts for seven days. On the first and seventh days of this feast, they were to hold a sacred assembly and these were considered to be Sabbath rests, a convocation or a high holy day (though not traditionally on the Saturday Sabbath, but in relation to the feasts), where no work was done, and they were to eat bread made without leaven or unleavened bread for the entire seven days of this feast, as well as present offerings by fire unto the Lord.

This feast corresponds to the three days and three nights that Jesus was in the grave. Many scholars have differing opinions as to the exact dates and how they relate to our current calendar. The Word of God declares that Jesus would be in the earth for three days and three nights, which challenges the Church's traditional thinking that Jesus died on Friday night. Some scholars believe that he died on Thursday night according to the customs within the feasts as well as Jewish traditions of the Old Testament, which supports the scriptural validity of Matthew 12:40.

⁴⁰ For as Jonah was three days and three nights in the belly of a huge fish, so the Son of Man will be three days and three nights in the heart of the earth.

Matthew 12:40

I believe the Manna was a Heavenly type of this Unleavened bread, which contained no yeast (sin). Remember the Manna when it first came down to the Israelites?

¹⁴ When the dew was gone, thin flakes like frost on the ground appeared on the desert floor. ¹⁵ When the Israelites saw it, they said to each other, "What is it?" For they did not know what it was. Moses said to them, "It is the bread the LORD has given you to eat. ¹⁶ This is what the LORD has commanded: 'Each one is to gather as much as he needs. Take an omer for each person you have in your tent.' "¹⁷ The Israelites did as they were told; some gathered much, some little. ¹⁸ And when they measured it by the omer, he who gathered much did not have too much, and he who gathered little did not have too little. Each one gathered as much as he needed.¹⁹ Then Moses said to them, "No one is to keep any of it until morning." ²⁰ However, some of them paid no attention to Moses; they kept part of it until morning, but it was full of maggots and began to smell. So Moses was angry with them.

Exodus 16:14-20

They were commanded to gather enough manna for one day, and those who rebelliously tried to reserve some for the next day found it to be ruined with maggots and smelly! But in preparation for the Sabbath, they were to collect a double portion, and found that the manna held in reserve did not ruin.

Jesus the Bread of Life

²⁶ Jesus answered, "I tell you the truth, you are looking for me, not because you saw miraculous signs but because you ate the loaves and had your fill. ²⁷ Do not work for food that spoils, but for food that endures to eternal life, which the Son of Man will give you. On him God the Father has placed his seal of approval." [31] Our forefathers ate the manna in the desert; as it is written: 'He gave them bread from heaven to eat.'" [32] Jesus said to them, "I tell you the truth, it is not Moses who has given you the bread from heaven, but it is my Father who gives you the true bread from heaven. [33] For the bread of God is he who comes down from heaven and gives life to the world." [34] "Sir," they said, "from now on give us this bread." [35] Then Jesus declared, "I am the bread of life. He who comes to me will never go hungry, and he who believes in me will never be thirsty.

John 6:26-27, 31-35

Jesus is the Manna from Heaven, the bread of life which is new every morning.

[33] *"For the bread of God is He who comes down from heaven and gives life to the world."*

John 6:33

[50] *"This is the bread which comes down from heaven, that one may eat of it and not die." [51] I am the living bread which came down from heaven. If anyone eats of this bread, he will live forever; and the bread that I shall give is My flesh, which I shall give for the life of the world."*

John 6:50-51

Jesus perfectly fulfilled this feast as he was the Bread without leaven which did not see decay. He was the Manna sent from Heaven to give life unto the world, and this symbolic period of eating the unleavened bread, represented the time that Jesus was in the grave, yet without sin (leaven). He was not left in the grave to decay! How could God provide Bread from Heaven that gave life if it saw decay in the grave? ***Selah***

[10] *because you will not abandon me to the grave, nor will you let your Holy One see decay.*

Psalm 16:10

³¹ Seeing what was ahead, he spoke of the resurrection of the Christ, that he was not abandoned to the grave, nor did his body see decay.

Acts 2:31

This period was also significant as it was the beginning of the Israelites' deliverance. It is believed by some that the first holy day was of course the day they physically left Egypt, and the seventh day was the crossing of the Red Sea. This was a historic crossing over from which they could not return, a period of bondage and slavery, a crossing from death to life as exemplified through Jesus death, and burial, and of course in His Resurrection, on the other side. It is also believed by many that when Joshua and the new generation crossed the Jordan River, it was during this same period of the Feast of Unleavened Bread. In fact Joshua commanded the people to consecrate themselves (Joshua 3:5) before they crossed over to the Promised Land, similar in spirit to the people removing leaven from their homes in preparation for the feast. Joshua 3:1- 17 details the account of Joshua and the next generation crossing the Jordan River. There are a few prophetic details we will look at as it relates to Jesus and his perfect fulfillment.

² After three days the officers went throughout the camp, ³ giving orders to the people: "When you see the ark of the covenant of the LORD your God, and the priests, who are Levites, carrying it, you are to move out from your positions and follow it. ⁴ Then you will know which way to go, since you have never been this way before. But keep a distance of about a thousand yards between you and the ark; do not go near it." ⁶ Joshua said to the priests, "Take up the ark of the covenant and pass on ahead of the people." So they took it up and went ahead of them. ⁷ And the LORD said to Joshua, "Today I will begin to exalt you in the eyes of all Israel, so they may know that I am with you as I was with Moses. ⁸ Tell the priests who carry the ark of the covenant: 'When you reach the edge of the Jordan's waters, go and stand in the river. ¹⁷ The priests who carried the ark of the covenant of the LORD stood firm on dry ground in the middle of the Jordan, while all

Israel passed by until the whole nation had completed the crossing on dry ground.
Joshua 3:2-4, 6-8, 17

Joshua commanded the priesthood to go and stand in the river, and in verse 17, they "stood firm on dry ground in the middle of the Jordan..." until the whole nation crossed over to the other side. In verses 3 and 4, Joshua told the people that when they saw the ark, they would know which way to go since they had never been that way before. This act of standing "the ground" in the river prophesied of the One who would complete this crossing for us to new life.

> [13] *Then Jesus came from Galilee to the Jordan to be baptized by John.* [14] *But John tried to deter him, saying, "I need to be baptized by you, and do you come to me?"* [15]*Jesus replied, "Let it be so now; it is proper for us to do this to fulfill all righteousness." Then John consented.* [16] *As soon as Jesus was baptized, he went up out of the water. At that moment heaven was opened, and he saw the Spirit of God descending like a dove and lighting on him.* [17] *And a voice from heaven said, "This is my Son, whom I love; with him I am well pleased."*
> *Matthew 3:13-17*

Jesus as our High Priest, the ark of His Glory, the ark of the Covenant, came from the other side of the Jordan, and went and stood in the middle of the river, and demonstrated the death, the burial, and the resurrection he was destined to fulfill. When the people saw this, they would know which way to go, "... since they had never been this way before." He is the way and the truth and the life, (John 14:6) and he came from the shores of the Promised Land, spiritual life, and stood the ground firmly demonstrating that in laying down his life, the people would ultimately cross over from spiritual death to life, from the wilderness of separation from God into the Promised Land of great harvest and freedom from sin. His journey to the cross was a done deal and settled under Heaven right there in the middle of the river, as he was not a man that could lie, thus sin and not be the sinless sacrifice required for salvation. This prophetic act was done for "...all righteousness to be fulfilled" in verse 15, and was signed, sealed and delivered by the voice of the Father, by the Heavens opening up and the Holy Spirit descending and lighting upon Him. All three persons of the Trinity were in perfect agreement and affirmed the transfer from the Old Covenant to the New Covenant. What a Historic moment for the Kingdom of God!

The Feast of Firstfruits

The Feast of Firstfruits obviously speaks of the Resurrection of our Lord Jesus Christ and occurs on the second day of the Feast of Unleavened Bread. This feast corresponds to the first day of the barley harvest, which was planted in winter, in which an omer or sheaf of this first grain is waived as an offering before the Lord by the priest. It also signifies the Lord bringing His people into their promised land, and in thanks offering up this first portion of their harvest to the Lord. It is the first day of the week, a work day, or Sunday, which also refers to the Day of Resurrection the church observes.

> [7] *Saying, The Son of man must be delivered into the hands of sinful men, and be crucified, and the third day rise again.*
>
> *Luke 24:7*

It is also the first day by which the days are counted toward the next feast.

> [29] *For those God foreknew he also predestined to be conformed to the likeness of his Son, that he might be the firstborn among many brothers.*
>
> *Romans 8:29*

> [18] *And he is the head of the body, the church; he is the beginning and the firstborn from among the dead, so that in everything he might have the supremacy*
>
> *Colossians 1:18*

> [23] *to the church of the firstborn, whose names are written in heaven. You have come to God, the judge of all men, to the spirits of righteous men made perfect*
>
> *Hebrews 12:23*

> *⁴ Grace and peace to you from him who is, and who was, and who is to come, and from the seven spirits before his throne, ⁵ and from Jesus Christ, who is the faithful witness, the firstborn from the dead, and the ruler of the kings of the earth.*
>
> *Revelation 1:4-5*

Jesus perfectly fulfilled this as the first of the resurrected ones, the One who overcame death and hell with the promise of resurrection to all those believe upon Him. He is truly the first of the Harvest in our Promised Land, as we have crossed over from death in to Life in Christ, with many more souls to come into the Kingdom. He is the firstborn spirit of life that is exchanged for the dead spirit we all inherited from Adam. As He exchanged the perishable (death) for the imperishable (eternal life), he offers the same to all of those who believe on him. It is interesting that he made this exchange while in the earth, and not just when he went into Heaven, but exhibited his Glorified body before many witnesses, admonishing them to not touch him in His current state in John 20:17 (he had not yet ascended to his Father). This is the last of the spring feasts, which also emphasize Jesus in his Priestly role.

The Feast of Weeks

This feast is most commonly referred to as the Feast of Pentecost (Shavuot) or the feast of the Harvest. It has also been named the Feast of Latter Firstfruits. This feast was originally named for the seven weeks that begin from the period of the Omer, or the Feast of Firstfruits, which is 49 days, with the Feast of Pentecost or Feast of Weeks beginning on the 50ᵗʰ day. Many Jews also believe that this was the exact time that God gave the Torah to Moses, which also bears the name *"Matin Torah"* or giving of the Law. This is one of three feasts called pilgrim feasts where every man was commanded to appear before the Lord in Jerusalem and bring an offering, the other two being the Feast of Unleavened Bread and the Feast of Tabernacles (Deut. 16:16). This is also one of the feasts that Solomon regularly observed (2 Chronicles 8:13) and possibly during the time of Ezekiel's vision on the Kebar River in Ezekiel 1.

The Feast of Weeks is the first and only summer feast, and corresponds to the second day of the Church. On this 50th day, they were to offer the new grain or the firstfruits of the wheat harvest. This was to be a very joyful feast and they were also to offer animal sacrifices. Traditional observance of this feast begins with the reading of the Torah as well as the book of Ruth, and also includes reciting blessings, feasting on dairy delights, possibly referring to the promised land of Milk and Honey, adorning their homes with greenery as related to the harvest and the reading of the Torah, and attending Shavuot services.

The exciting significance of this Feast is related to Jesus and His Church. Jesus appeared to many witnesses for about 40 days where he commissioned them to spread the good news of Jesus Christ to the ends of the earth.

> [16] *Then the eleven disciples went away into Galilee, into a mountain where Jesus had appointed them.* [17] *And when they saw him, they worshipped him: but some doubted.* [18] *And Jesus came and spake unto them, saying, All power is given unto me in heaven and in earth.* [19] *Go ye therefore, and teach all nations, baptizing them in the name of the Father, and of the Son, and of the Holy Ghost:*[20] *Teaching them to observe all things whatsoever I have commanded you: and, lo, I am with you always, even unto the end of the world. Amen.*
>
> *Matthew 28:16-20*

In Acts 1, Jesus admonished his disciples to wait for something very special, a gift that Jesus requested from His Father.

> [4] *And, being assembled together with them, commanded them that they should not depart from Jerusalem, but wait for the promise of the Father, which, saith he, ye have heard of me.*[5] *For John truly baptized with water; but ye shall be baptized with the Holy Ghost not many days hence.* [8] *But ye shall receive power, after that the Holy Ghost is come upon you: and ye shall be witnesses unto me both in Jerusalem, and in all Judaea, and in Samaria,*

and unto the uttermost part of the earth. ⁹ And when he had spoken these things, while they beheld, he was taken up; and a cloud received him out of their sight.

Acts 1:4-5, 8-9

This precious gift of the promised Holy Spirit as received by the believer was the ***"power when the Holy Spirit comes on you"*** which would enable them to be witnesses to the entire world, literally turning the world upside down! Let's see this first day of Pentecost, which occurred exactly 50 days from the Feast of Firstfruits.

The Holy Spirit Comes at Pentecost

¹ When the day of Pentecost came, they were all together in one place. ² Suddenly a sound like the blowing of a violent wind came from heaven and filled the whole house where they were sitting. ³ They saw what seemed to be tongues of fire that separated and came to rest on each of them. ⁴ All of them were filled with the Holy Spirit and began to speak in other tongues as the Spirit enabled them. ⁵ Now there were staying in Jerusalem God-fearing Jews from every nation under heaven. ⁶ When they heard this sound, a crowd came together in bewilderment, because each one heard them speaking in his own language.⁷ Utterly amazed, they asked: "Are not all these men who are speaking Galileans? ⁸ Then how is it that each of us hears them in his own native language?

Acts 2:1-8

The Word of God declares this to be the exact day when the Holy Spirit came blowing through with a violent wind and tongues of fire above every head! It is interesting that in verse 5, God had already assembled witnesses to this event, **"Now there were staying in Jerusalem God-fearing Jews from every nation under heaven."** God wanted to personally publish his own Word and provide news coverage that would circle the globe, and of course because they all spoke in different languages, they heard the Good News in every language. I believe the Holy Spirit is still quite capable and willing to send his servants around the world with a supernatural crash course in the native tongue! Of course, in verse

13, they assumed these men must be drunk, possibly because they were drinking of a new wine! Peter then addresses the crowd in a new found boldness, empowered by the Holy Spirit in verses 14-40. Look what he says in verses 38-39.

> [38] *Peter replied, "Repent and be baptized, every one of you, in the name of Jesus Christ for the forgiveness of your sins. And you will receive the gift of the Holy Spirit.* [39] *The promise is for you and your children and for all who are far off—for all whom the Lord our God will call."*
>
> *Acts 1:38-39*

This gift is promised not only to that first eye witness generation but to their children, which represents all generations to this day. And here was the fruit of that first outpouring of the Holy Spirit in verses 41-47.

> [41] *Those who accepted his message were baptized, and about three thousand were added to their number that day.*
>
> *The Fellowship of the Believers*
>
> [42] *They devoted themselves to the apostles' teaching and to the fellowship, to the breaking of bread and to prayer.* [43] *Everyone was filled with awe, and many wonders and miraculous signs were done by the apostles.* [44] *All the believers were together and had everything in common.* [45] *Selling their possessions and goods, they gave to anyone as he had need.* [46] *Every day they continued to meet together in the temple courts. They broke bread in their homes and ate together with glad and sincere hearts,* [47] *praising God and enjoying the favor of all the people. And the Lord added to their number daily those who were being saved.*
>
> *Acts 1:41-47*

All previous feasts were celebrated with sacrifices of fire. This was a feast of joy in receiving his most precious gift, the Holy Spirit. God brought His own Fire through the Holy Spirit manifested in tongues of fire and a violent wind of Heaven's change! And the fruit was that three thousand were added the first day, and many were added daily to His Newly birthed Church! If Jesus was the First Fruit, this would explain the name of this feast being the Latter Firstfruits and the firstborn of many brethren! The first fruits could also refer to the fruits of the spirit in Galatians 5:21-23, *22 "But the fruit of the Spirit is love, joy, peace, patience, kindness, goodness, faithfulness,23 gentleness and self-control. Against such things there is no law."*

I believe the culmination of this Second Day Phenomenon was the visitation at Azusa Street. I believe the Holy Spirit wants to still visit us in this magnificence if we would freely receive his Gift to us, the gift promised us by the Son of God from his own Father. How great our witness would be! Just as when he first came upon us, He emboldened us with His Power from on High, and we would appear to be different men and women of God, with the Church spreading like a raging wildfire! The Day of Pentecost was the first fruit of the Harvest, and we will see a fruition of the Great Harvest to come. The Promise of Haggai 2:9 applies here.

> *9 'The glory of this present house will be greater than the glory of the former house,' says the LORD Almighty. 'And in this place I will grant peace,'declares the LORD Almighty."*
>
> *Haggai 2:9*
>
> *23 Be glad, O people of Zion, rejoice in the LORD your God, for he has given you the autumn rains in righteousness. He sends you abundant showers, both autumn and spring rains, as before.*
>
> *Joel 2:23*
>
> *2 After two days he will revive us; on the third day he will restore us, that we may live in his presence.*
>
> *Hosea 6:2*
>
> *3 Then shall we know, if we follow on to know the LORD: his going forth is prepared as the morning; and he shall come unto us as the rain, as the latter and former rain unto the earth.*
>
> *Hosea 6:3*

The Feast of Trumpets

> *23 Then the Lord spoke to Moses, saying, 24 "Speak to the children of Israel, saying: 'In the seventh month, on the first day of the month, you shall have a sabbath-rest, a memorial of blowing of trumpets, a holy convocation. 25 You shall do no customary work on it; and you shall offer an offering made by fire to the Lord.'"*
>
> *Leviticus 23:23-25*

The feast of Trumpets, also Rosh Hashanah, ushers in the fall feasts, which emphasize the Kingship of Jesus Christ and his coming Kingdom. This feast today begins with the blowing of the Shofar at the Western Wall. The Lord declares this to be a Sabbath rest for the people and a memorial of blowing of trumpets, I believe for all that God has done for His people and all that He will continue to do for them. The trumpets were used to call a Holy Assembly or to accompany the Armies of the Lord as instruments of warfare. The trumpet also announced the procession of the King. Many believe that this will actually be the sound of the trumpet which raptures the Church out of the tribulation filled world!

> *14 We believe that Jesus died and rose again and so we believe that God will bring with Jesus those who have fallen asleep in him. 15 According to the Lord's own word, we tell you that we who are still alive, who are left till the coming of the Lord, will certainly not precede those who have fallen asleep. 16 For the Lord himself will come down from heaven, with a loud command, with the voice of the archangel and with the trumpet call of God, and the dead in Christ will rise first. 17 After that, we who are still alive and are left will be caught up together with them in the clouds to meet the Lord in the air. And so we will be with the Lord forever.*
>
> *1 Thessalonians 4:14-17*

What a promise from the Lord! Of course there is no timetable attached to this promise, and many debate as to when this will occur in light of current events. This also coincides with Jesus promise to us in John 14.

> *2 In my Father's house are many rooms; if it were not so,*
> *I would have told you. I am going there to prepare a place*
> *for you. 3 And if I go and prepare a place for you, I will*
> *come back and take you to be with me that you also may*
> *be where I am.*
>
> John 14:2-3

Many also believe that at a future Feast of Trumpets, this will restart the end-time prophetic 70th week, spoken of by Daniel, the beginning of the end, or the Great Tribulation, where Israel enters into a treaty of false peace, dividing up Jerusalem and their land, only to be deceived by the evil one. This may also spark the great end-time revival with a praying Church in desperation as spoken by Joel in Joel 2:28-32.

The Day of the LORD

> *28 "And afterward, I will pour out my Spirit on all people.*
> *Your sons and daughters will prophesy, your old men*
> *will dream dreams, your young men will see visions. 29*
> *Even on my servants, both men and women, I will pour*
> *out my Spirit in those days. 30 I will show wonders in*
> *the heavens and on the earth, blood and fire and billows*
> *of smoke. 31 The sun will be turned to darkness and the*
> *moon to blood before the coming of the great and dreadful*
> *day of the LORD. 32 And everyone who calls on the name*
> *of the LORD will be saved; for on Mount Zion and in*
> *Jerusalem there will be deliverance, as the LORD has*
> *said, among the survivors whom the LORD calls.*
>
> Joel 2:28-32

The Day of Atonement

The Day of Atonement, also known as Yom Kippur is considered by many Jews to be the most Holy Day of all. He established this special day in Leviticus 23:26-32.

Day of Atonement

> ²⁶ *The LORD said to Moses,* ²⁷ *"The tenth day of this seventh month is the Day of Atonement. Hold a sacred assembly and deny yourselves, and present an offering made to the LORD by fire.* ²⁸ *Do no work on that day, because it is the Day of Atonement, when atonement is made for you before the LORD your God.* ²⁹ *Anyone who does not deny himself on that day must be cut off from his people.* ³⁰ *I will destroy from among his people anyone who does any work on that day.* ³¹ *You shall do no work at all. This is to be a lasting ordinance for the generations to come, wherever you live.* ³² *It is a sabbath of rest for you, and you must deny yourselves. From the evening of the ninth day of the month until the following evening you are to observe your sabbath."*
>
> Leviticus 23:26-32

Also in Leviticus 16, after the death of Aaron's sons, Nadab and Abihu, in Leviticus 10, the Lord establishes this day once a year for the high priest to make atonement not only for his own sins but for the sins of the entire community.

> ² *The LORD said to Moses: "Tell your brother Aaron not to come whenever he chooses into the Most Holy Place behind the curtain in front of the atonement cover on the ark, or else he will die, because I appear in the cloud over the atonement cover.*
>
> Leviticus 16:2

The Lord gave very specific instructions as a lasting ordinance of the priesthood of Aaron, that they would be able to enter this Most Holy Place without incurring death. They were not to casually go before the Atonement Cover of the Ark, **"because I appear in the cloud over the atonement cover."** This ceremony was to be performed once a year, for the sins of the previous year, where the priest would deny himself. Many observe this solemn day without eating or drinking even water. It is a day that reflects the Days when the Books are sealed, the Final Judgment and is considered to be a last appeal before the Final

Judgment. Jesus as our High Priest also demonstrated this requirement to his followers.

> *²³ Then he said to them all: "If anyone would come after me, he must deny himself and take up his cross daily and follow me.*
>
> *Luke 9:23*

Of course Jesus as our High Priest was the first to deny Himself and to take up His Cross. He denied Himself in the Garden of Gethsamane, *⁴² "Saying, Father, if thou be willing, remove this cup from me: nevertheless not my will, but thine, be done." (Luke 22:42)* Paul also admonished us in Romans 12 in the same pattern as Jesus.

> *¹ Therefore, I urge you, brothers, in view of God's mercy, to offer your bodies as living sacrifices, holy and pleasing to God —this is your spiritual act of worship. ² Do not conform any longer to the pattern of this world, but be transformed by the renewing of your mind. Then you will be able to test and approve what God's will is —his good, pleasing and perfect will.*
>
> *Romans 12:1-2*

Jesus as our High Priest perfectly fulfilled this Day of Atonement by offering up Himself as the sacrificial Lamb and making the way into this Holy of Holies which was previously forbidden to all.

> *¹⁹ Therefore, brothers, since we have confidence to enter the Most Holy Place by the blood of Jesus, ²⁰ by a new and living way opened for us through the curtain, that is, his body, ²¹ and since we have a great priest over the house of God,*
>
> *Hebrews 10:19-21*

He was the Scapegoat by which the sin of the world was placed upon Him and rejected by all. He writes our names in the Lamb's Book of Life and has personally blotted out all our transgressions with the ink pen of His Precious Red Blood.

²⁷ *Nothing impure will ever enter it, nor will anyone who does what is shameful or deceitful, but only those whose names are written in the Lamb's book of life.*

Revelation 21:27

How phenomenal it is that our God would speak of the One who would fulfill every Holy Day and Feast through His Son, and then send Him into the World to perfectly fulfill every last word spoken about Him!

I will go in depth into the final feast, the Feast of Tabernacles in the next chapter. There are two other festivals I want to mention which are traditionally observed by the Jewish people, both of which are post-Mosaic and in celebration of their deliverance as a people. These are Purim and Channukah.

The Festival of Purim is a celebration of the deliverance of the Israelite people through Esther as detailed in the Book of Esther, also known as the Megillah (or scroll). The name Purim means "lots" which was the way Haman determined the day in which to annihilate the Jews. This festival is celebrated on the 14th day in the last month of the Hebrew year, the month of Adar, or in leap years Adar II (they add this month) and is usually a month before Passover, in the month of March.

As the Book of Esther records, Esther (her Gentile name, Hadassah, her Jewish name) was a Jewish exile from the Kingdom of Judah, now living under Persian rule in the walled city of Shushan (Susa). Under the King's orders, Esther, along with other maidens, was brought into the palace of King Ahasuerus as a part of his harem, in a contest to be the Queen of all the land. The King found favor with her and Esther was crowned as Queen in the land. Though Jewish by birth, she hid her nationality from the King, according to her uncle Mordecai's advice. Mordecai was a scribe in the palace and a righteous man. The story continues when Haman, royal vizier to the King, wanted to destroy Mordecai because he would not bow to Haman. Haman concocted a scheme about a certain people in the land that would not obey the King, the Jews, which would ultimately destroy not only Mordecai, but Esther the Queen as well as annihilate the entire Jewish nation.

Esther goes on a three day fast before approaching the King. (This three day fast called the Fast of Esther precedes the holiday.) It would mean Esther's death to go unannounced before the King according to the protocols of the land. She goes before the King to intercede on behalf of her people and intervene for the salvation of the Jewish people. The King gives the order that instead of the Jewish people to be destroyed, Haman would hang on the gallows he built for Mordecai. Thus Purim is a great festival, one of the most joyous and fun. It is observed by reading the Book of Esther, giving mutual gifts of food and drink, giving to the poor and a great feast of celebration. Other customs include performing plays or parodies and holding beauty contests. They are to be merry in their celebration.

The final festival is Channukah (Hannukah) or the Festival of Lights. This holiday is celebrated from the 25th day of Kislev, which is usually late November to late December. This is an eight day celebration commemorating the miraculous victory of the Jews and the rededication of the Jewish Temple after the Maccabean revolt in the second century BC. The Jews were under great persecution in the Greek empire and religious oppression. Their suffering was great as the leader Antiochus IV placed a Hellenistic priest in the Temple, massacred Jews, prohibited the practice of the Jewish religion, and desecrated the Temple by requiring the sacrifice of pigs on the altar, which was considered an abomination.

The revolt succeeded and the Maccabees, in their rededication of the Temple, had only enough oil to light the Menorah for one day. The miracle of which Hanukah is known for was that the oil lasted for eight days, thus the holiday became an eight day celebration, where one candle is lit each day until all are lit. The menorah has nine candles, the one in the middle is called the shammus, meaning servant, is at a different height, distinguished from the others, and is first lit. The first candle is placed to the right and after the prayers and blessings are recited, the shammus is used to light the first candle and then placed back in its holder. Each candle is added from right to left and the newest candle is first lit, as you pay honor to the newest first. There are other customs associated with this festival, such as the eating of fried foods, made with oil, and the traditional gift is the "gelt," the giving of small amounts of money, as well as other customs. These final two festivals as well as all the festivals celebrate the deliverance of the Jewish people and the great love God had for his people. After all, they are considered to be the "Apple of his Eye!"

Chapter 6

The Feast of Tabernacles

The Feast of Tabernacles is the last of the seven feasts the Lord through Moses established for his people to observe with celebration and with sacred assembly. This feast is also known as the Feast of Ingathering referring to the Harvest (Lev. 23:39, Ex. 23:16, Ex. 34:22), the Feast of Booths (Sukkot), when Israel dwelled in the wilderness in these booths, and is later singled out from all other feasts as the Feast or the Feast of the Lord (Jehovah). This feast is believed by many to be the only feast not yet fulfilled and the one that is the culmination of all the other feasts as well as the Great Harvest of all people and nations, also known as the Feast of the Gentile Nations (Zech. 14:20).

> 33 The LORD said to Moses, 34 "Say to the Israelites: 'On the fifteenth day of the seventh month the LORD's Feast of Tabernacles begins, and it lasts for seven days. 35 The first day is a sacred assembly; do no regular work. 36 For seven days present offerings made to the LORD by fire, and on the eighth day hold a sacred assembly and present an offering made to the LORD by fire. It is the closing assembly; do no regular work.37 (""These are the LORD's appointed feasts, which you are to proclaim as sacred assemblies for bringing offerings made to the LORD by fire—the burnt offerings and grain offerings, sacrifices and drink offerings required for each day. 38 These offerings are in addition to those for the LORD's Sabbaths and in addition to your gifts and whatever you have vowed and all the freewill offerings you give to the LORD.' ") 39 "'So beginning with the fifteenth day of the seventh month, after you have gathered the crops of the land, celebrate the festival to the LORD for seven days;

the first day is a day of rest, and the eighth day also is a day of rest. [40] On the first day you are to take choice fruit from the trees, and palm fronds, leafy branches and poplars, and rejoice before the LORD your God for seven days. [41] Celebrate this as a festival to the LORD for seven days each year. This is to be a lasting ordinance for the generations to come; celebrate it in the seventh month. [42] Live in booths for seven days: All native-born Israelites are to live in booths [43] so your descendants will know that I had the Israelites live in booths when I brought them out of Egypt. I am the LORD your God.'" [44] So Moses announced to the Israelites the appointed feasts of the LORD.

Leviticus 23:33-44

I was tempted to include only a portion of this entire section, but there is so much meat in this feast that is applicable to us today. The Jewish historian Josephus declares this feast to be the Holiest and greatest of all the Hebrew feasts. There are many facets of this feast both written and observed directly in scripture as well as the historical tradition later within the Temple in celebration of this feast. Let us first glean from the scripture in the establishment of this important feast.

I believe it is significant to note that the spring feasts begin with Passover on the 15th day of the first month and the Feast of Tabernacles begins on the 15th day of the seventh month, (around October) at its full moon, or full strength. Where the Sabbath was the seventh day as related to the week, this feast was the seventh month as related to the year, signifying the end of the sacred year as well as the agricultural year. (It marked the change of seasons, the approach of rain and the winter equinox.) Seven as we know is the number of God's completion or fullness and it appears many times throughout this feast. The feast lasts for seven days, they were to live in booths for seven days, and seven was the number divisible in each of the animal sacrifices, i.e. 70 bullocks total, etc. as specified in Numbers 29:12-40. Interestingly, the number of bullocks offered began at 13 on the first day and decreased each day until on the seventh day, there was only 7 required for sacrifice, while the rams and year old male lambs remained the same, all divisible in total by seven. Also in Deuteronomy 31:10-11, Moses declared that at the end of every seven years, in the year of cancelling debts, during the Feast of Tabernacles, the law would be read, also known as the Rejoicing in the Law.

> [10] *Then Moses commanded them: "At the end of every seven years, in the year for canceling debts, during the Feast of Tabernacles,* [11] *when all Israel comes to appear before the LORD your God at the place he will choose, you shall read this law before them in their hearing.*
>
> *Deuteronomy 31:10-11*

The first day and the eighth day were to be sacred assemblies and no work was to be done. Each day had apportioned sacrifices they were to observe, including the animal sacrifices, the grain offerings, the drink offerings, and the fellowship offerings which are more clearly described in Numbers 29:12- 40 as Moses instructs the priesthood on the requirements of this feast.

In Leviticus 23:40, the people are instructed to take choice fruit, palm fronds, leafy branches, and poplars to rejoice before the Lord for the seven days of this festival, most believe they carried these in their hands as part of the worship. In verse 41 he declares this to be a lasting ordinance for generations to come. I believe we are included with those future generations! In verses 42-43, he concludes with the introduction of the booths, in which they were to live for seven days, constructed of their own hands from boughs of living trees. This was a reminder for the Israelites' descendants of their fathers who lived in booths in the wilderness and of the faithfulness of their God and his provision for them.

> [13] *Celebrate the Feast of Tabernacles for seven days after you have gathered the produce of your threshing floor and your winepress.* [14] *Be joyful at your Feast— you, your sons and daughters, your menservants and maidservants, and the Levites, the aliens, the fatherless and the widows who live in your towns.* [15] *For seven days celebrate the Feast to the LORD your God at the place the LORD will choose. For the LORD your God will bless you in all your harvest and in all the work of your hands, and your joy will be complete.* [16] *Three times a year all*

> *your men must appear before the LORD your God at the place he will choose: at the Feast of Unleavened Bread, the Feast of Weeks and the Feast of Tabernacles. No man should appear before the LORD empty-handed:* [17] *Each of you must bring a gift in proportion to the way the LORD your God has blessed you.*
>
> *Deuteronomy 16:13-17*

In this scripture, Moses further emphasizes the gathering of their harvest and the joy that should be experienced during this feast, and in verse 15 he promises that God will bless their harvest and their work and their joy will be complete. Also, he commands this to be one of three required feasts that every man will appear before the Lord, the Feast of Unleavened Bread, the Feast of Weeks, and the Feast of Tabernacles. Every man is required to bring a gift in proportion to the way the Lord has blessed him. I believe this is how God wants us to bring our gifts, not just a tenth but a joyful gift in proportion to the Blessing of the Lord in our lives.

As you can see, there is much to glean from this feast, both from the scriptural establishment of this feast through Moses, and the historic traditions that accompanied this feast, later in the ceremonies associated with the Temple, obviously post-Mosaic. Much of what the Jewish nation did was a prophetic gesture and displayed many aspects of the Christ who was to come, and who now has. During the first night watch, the altar for the burnt offerings to be made was cleansed, and after midnight, the gates of the Temple were thrown open. They then examined all of the animals to be sacrificed before the morning sacrifices began. Two important ceremonies of the Feast of Tabernacles are the pouring out of water and the illumination of the Temple.

The priest accompanied by joyous worshippers went to the Pool of Siloam where he drew water into a golden pitcher, about 2 pints. However on the Sabbath, they drew water from a golden vessel within the Temple which had been carried from Siloam the day before. This is very similar to the way the Israelites gathered manna enough for one day, and for the Sabbath gathered two portions which were preserved during the Sabbath day of rest. This was done while the morning sacrifices were being prepared, as another priest journeyed to the Kidron Valley to gather willow branches which were assembled on both sides of the altar, bending over as a leafy canopy. The priest who collected the water came in through the "Water-gate" which was named as part of this ceremony, as the priests blew a threefold blast from their trumpets. The priests ascended the altar where there were two silver basins with narrow holes, the eastern side was a little larger intended for the wine, and the western side was for the water to be poured. The wine of the drink offering was poured on the east side at the same time as the water was being poured on the west side which led to the basin of the altar.

I believe this simultaneous pouring out of wine and water symbolized when Jesus was pierced with the sword in his side and out came blood and water (John 19:34). The wine symbolized the blood of Jesus, the wine of the New Covenant and the blood that was shed on our behalf to provide salvation. The water symbolized the Living Water whom Jesus declared himself to be (John 4:14), *"...a spring of water welling up to eternal life..."* and in Isaiah 12:3, *"With joy you shall draw water from the wells of salvation."* I am also reminded of the time when Jesus washed his disciples' feet, which demonstrated the heart of the servant. This reminds me of a worship song the Lord had given me about 7 years ago, called "Come and Drink of My Worship."

Come and drink of my worship
Come and taste my adoration
Come and sip of my Love for you
For I am poured out like water before you
Broken and spilled out before you.

The water also symbolizes the pouring out of the Holy Spirit, both in the Day of Pentecost in Acts 2: 1-13, as well as in Joel 2:28-32, where he says he will pour out His Spirit on all flesh.

After the pouring of the wine and the water, the Temple music began with the singing of Psalms 113-118, (the 'Hallel') accompanied by flutes, except on the Sabbath and the first day of the feast when flutes were not allowed to be played. As the choirs sang, the worshippers shook their *lulavs*, or palm branches towards the altar. This also reminds me of Jesus triumphal entry into the city of Jerusalem upon a humble donkey, when the people gathered palm branches to meet him, and spread them out before him (John 12:12-15, Matt.21:1-11). This is also the eternal glimpse of worship in Heaven.

> *⁹ After this I looked and there before me was a great multitude that no one could count, from every nation, tribe, people and language, standing before the throne and in front of the Lamb. They were wearing white robes and were holding palm branches in their hands.*
>
> *Revelation 7:9*

Also, as part of the ceremony of the festive sacrifices, the priests would sing and form a procession, making a circuit of the altar every day for seven days, while on the seventh day, "the great day of the feast," they circled the altar seven times. This was in remembrance of the miracle God performed when the walls of Jericho fell down. This of course perfectly corresponds to the pouring out of water, when the Lord says that he will pour out his Spirit upon all flesh. There will be no walls between peoples, or within the church, no walls of separation nor division. The Jewish nation was a priestly nation, and I believe this prophetic act was not just about their nation but as the walls came down for them in Jericho, so the walls could come down for all Gentile nations as well. This feast is not only connected to Israel but also to all the Gentile nations as prophesied in Zechariah 14:16-21, and is also known as the Feast of the Gentile Nations.

> *¹⁶ Then the survivors from all the nations that have attacked Jerusalem will go up year after year to worship the King, the LORD Almighty, and to celebrate the Feast of Tabernacles. ¹⁷ If any of the peoples of the earth do not go up to Jerusalem to worship the King, the LORD Almighty, they will have no rain. ¹⁸ If the Egyptian people do not go up and take part, they will have no rain. The LORD will bring on them the plague he inflicts on the nations that do not go up to celebrate the Feast of Tabernacles. ¹⁹ This will be the punishment of Egypt and the punishment of all the nations that do not go up to celebrate the Feast of Tabernacles. ²⁰ On that day HOLY TO THE LORD will be inscribed on the bells of the horses, and the cooking pots in the LORD's house will be*

like the sacred bowls in front of the altar. ²¹ Every pot in Jerusalem and Judah will be holy to the LORD Almighty, and all who come to sacrifice will take some of the pots and cook in them. And on that day there will no longer be a Canaanite in the house of the LORD Almighty.

Zechariah 14:16-21

This aspect of the feast may also correspond to the prophecy declared in Haggai 2:9, and may be the singular reason that we are experiencing the shaking of the nations, in that His Glory may once again fill His House. This Glory is not just for the Jewish House as in the former house, but the Gentile House as well, which would be the latter house, the Church, "the desired of all nations shall come," in Haggai 2:7.

⁶ For thus saith the LORD of hosts; Yet once, it is a little while, and I will shake the heavens, and the earth, and the sea, and the dry land; ⁷ And I will shake all nations, and the desire of all nations shall come: and I will fill this house with glory, saith the LORD of hosts. ⁸ The silver is mine, and the gold is mine, saith the LORD of hosts. ⁹ The glory of this latter house shall be greater than of the former, saith the LORD of hosts: and in this place will I give peace, saith the LORD of hosts.

Haggai 2:6-9 KJV

Jesus and the Feast of Tabernacles

In John 7, we learn that Jesus actually participated in the ceremonies associated with the Feast of Tabernacles. In John 7:6 and 10, Jesus' own brothers, who did not yet believe in him, urged Jesus to go up to the Feast, yet Jesus declared that his time had not yet come. His brothers went ahead, and Jesus went also, but in private. In verse 14, Jesus went up to the Temple and taught halfway through the Feast to the amazement of all the people who marveled at his teaching. On the final day of the great Feast, Jesus' prophetic time had come. Listen to what He said, I believe, after the priests poured out the wine and the water, and possibly after the priests made their final circuit around the altar after the sacrifice.

[37] On the last and greatest day of the Feast, Jesus stood and said in a loud voice, "If anyone is thirsty, let him come to me and drink. [38] Whoever believes in me, as the Scripture has said, streams of living water will flow from within him." [39] By this he meant the Spirit, whom those who believed in him were later to receive. Up to that time the Spirit had not been given, since Jesus had not yet been glorified.

John 7:37-39

Instead of going to the Pool of Siloam, Jesus declared that they should come to Him in order that **"....streams of living water will flow from within him**." In verse 39, John explains that for those who believed in Jesus, they would receive this living water which was the Spirit that had not yet been given, as Jesus had not yet fulfilled his destiny as Messiah. The worshippers were stunned by this announcement, even grasping the reference Jesus inferred with the Feast. Many questioned if he was a prophet or even the Christ to the upset of the religious leaders present.

Jesus also extends this invitation to a Samaritan who was not completely Jewish, but partly Gentile. He offers her up a drink from Himself that she would never thirst again, one that would bring her eternal life. She also references going up to Jerusalem to worship in verse 19, I believe, in association with the Feast where they drew the water from the Pool of Siloam.

[7] When a Samaritan woman came to draw water, Jesus said to her, "Will you give me a drink?"[8] (His disciples had gone into the town to buy food.) [9] The Samaritan woman said to him, "You are a Jew and I am a Samaritan woman. How can you ask me for a drink?" (For Jews do not associate with Samaritans.) [10] Jesus answered her, "If you knew the gift of God and who it is that asks you for a drink, you would have asked him and he would have given you living water."[11] "Sir," the woman said, "you have nothing to draw with and the well is deep. Where can you get this living water? [12] Are you greater than our father Jacob, who gave us the well and drank from it himself, as did also his sons and his flocks and herds?"

¹³ Jesus answered, "Everyone who drinks this water will be thirsty again, ¹⁴ but whoever drinks the water I give him will never thirst. Indeed, the water I give him will become in him a spring of water welling up to eternal life." ¹⁵ The woman said to him, "Sir, give me this water so that I won't get thirsty and have to keep coming here to draw water."

John 4:7-15

Could this Living Water be the same prophetic picture as the River that flows from Ezekiel's not yet constructed Temple? **Selah** It flows from the altar out of the Temple belonging to the Jews and out into the world, giving life to all that come in contact with it.

The River From the Temple

¹ The man brought me back to the entrance of the temple, and I saw water coming out from under the threshold of the temple toward the east (for the temple faced east). The water was coming down from under the south side of the temple, south of the altar. ² He then brought me out through the north gate and led me around the outside to the outer gate facing east, and the water was flowing from the south side. ³ As the man went eastward with a measuring line in his hand, he measured off a thousand cubits and then led me through water that was ankle-deep. ⁴ He measured off another thousand cubits and led me through water that was knee-deep. He measured off another thousand and led me through water that was up to the waist. ⁵ He measured off another thousand, but now it was a river that I could not cross, because the water had risen and was deep enough to swim in—a river that no one could cross. ⁶ He asked me, "Son of man, do you see this?" Then he led me back to the bank of the river. ⁷ When I arrived there, I saw a great number of trees on each side of the river. ⁸ He said to me, "This water flows toward the eastern region and goes down into the Arabah, where it enters the Sea. When it empties into the Sea, the water there becomes fresh. ⁹ Swarms of living creatures will live wherever the river flows. There will be large numbers of fish, because this water flows there and makes the salt water fresh; so where the river flows everything will live.

Ezekiel 47:1-9

I believe this Life giving River flowing from the Temple is Jesus, the one poured out from the Jewish nation to give new life to the lost sea of humanity, to both Jewish and Gentile believers alike. This is also the source from which the Spirit will be poured out upon all flesh in Joel 2:28. This is an ever unfolding revelation and the more I dive in, the sweeter the water becomes!

Let us further visit the significance of the Pool of Siloam. Jesus encountered a man who was born blind, whom he healed on the Sabbath in John 9.

¹ And as Jesus passed by, he saw a man which was blind from his birth.² And his disciples asked him, saying, Master, who did sin, this man, or his parents, that he was born blind?³ Jesus answered, Neither hath this man sinned, nor his parents: but that the works of God should be made manifest in him.⁴ I must work the works of him that sent me, while it is day: the night cometh, when no man can work.⁵ As long as I am in the world, I am the light of the world.⁶ When he had thus spoken, he spat on the ground, and made clay of the spittle, and he anointed the eyes of the blind man with the clay, ⁷ And said unto him, Go, wash in the pool of Siloam, (which is by interpretation, Sent.) He went his way therefore, and washed, and came seeing.

John 9:1-7 KJV

Jesus healed this blind man and told him to go wash in the Pool of Siloam. Before he sent the man, Jesus declared in verse 5, **"...I am the light of the world."** Jesus was not only the Life giving water that brought healing to this man, but also the Light of the World, who came to heal not just the man with natural blindness, but all of spiritual blindness, including the religious leaders blinded by their own agendas. This healing also alluded to the Feast of Tabernacles. There is one more aspect of the ceremonies of the Feast we want to glean from, the ceremonies in the Court of Women.

As the first day of the feast came to a close, the worshippers descended to the Court of the Women where great preparations were made. There were four candelabras, each with four golden bowls, with four ladders resting against them, with four youths who were priestly in their descent. They each held a pitcher of oil from which they filled each of the bowls. Retired breeches of the priests served as the wicks of these lamps. All of the courts of Jerusalem were said to be lit up by the light of 'the house of water-pouring.' Certain men, called the Chassidim and Men of Deed danced with flaming torches before the people, singing hymns and songs, while the musical Levites accompanied them with the instruments used in Temple worship. These Levites stood upon the fifteen steps which led down from the Court of Israel to the Court of women. As the two priests blew a threefold trumpet blast, they would advance, with periodic trumpet blasts, until they reached the gate of the east, the Beautiful Gate. As they reached the east gate they turned towards the west, facing the Holy Place and in penitent form said, "Our fathers who were in this place, they turned their back upon the Sanctuary of Jehovah, and their faces toward the east, and they worshipped the rising sun; but as for us, our eyes are towards the Lord." Thus the children were repenting for the idolatry of the fathers, yet turning back toward their God.

I believe that both the pouring out of water and the Illumination of the Temple were one in the same, found in the fulfillment of Jesus' life both being poured out for salvation and giving light to the darkness of the world that all men could see. As Jesus is the Light of the world, He has placed the candle of the Lord within each one of us that we may so shine before men, and all will be drawn to the Light of His Flame, fueled by the Oil of the Holy Spirit. My heart is singing, "This little light of mine, I'm gonna let it shine...Hide it under a bushel, NO, I'm gonna let it shine!" I am also reminded of the 5 wise virgins awaiting the approach of their bridegroom, who kept their oil lit in their lamps in Matthew 25:1-13.

Obviously these two very important ceremonies of the Feast of Tabernacles occurred within the Temple and were after the original establishing of the Feast through Moses. They were very prophetic of the one to come, the Messiah, the Christ, who would pour his life out for our salvation and bring light to a world of spiritual darkness.

Other significant events occurred during the Feast of Tabernacles according to Jewish tradition. They believed that the pillar of cloud by day and the pillar of fire by night appeared on the fifteenth of the seventh month (Tishri), the first day of the feast. They also believe that Moses descended from the Mount on that same day, detailing the Tabernacle of God to be built, as well as delivering the Law. The most significant event that occurred during the Feast of Tabernacles was at the dedication of Solomon's Temple, where the Shekinah Glory came from Heaven and took up residence in the Holy of Holies above the Mercy Seat.

> [1] *When Solomon finished praying, fire came down from heaven and consumed the burnt offering and the sacrifices, and the glory of the LORD filled the temple.* [2] *The priests could not enter the temple of the LORD because the glory of the LORD filled it.*[3] *When all the Israelites saw the fire coming down and the glory of the LORD above the temple, they knelt on the pavement with their faces to the ground, and they worshiped and gave thanks to the LORD, saying, "He is good; his love endures forever."*
>
> *2 Chronicles 7:1-3*

If the glory of the former house, Solomon's Temple, was so magnificent when the Glory of Heaven was ushered into its residence, the Holy of Holies, how much more will the glory of this latter house be?

> [9] *The glory of this latter house shall be greater than of the former, saith the LORD of hosts: and in this place will I give peace, saith the LORD of hosts.*
>
> *Haggai 2:9 KJV*

Of course we also see this same scene in the Heavenly realm of Revelation 7.

> [9] *After this I looked and there before me was a great multitude that no one could count, from every nation,*

tribe, people and language, standing before the throne and in front of the Lamb. They were wearing white robes and were holding palm branches in their hands. [10] And they cried out in a loud voice: "Salvation belongs to our God, who sits on the throne, and to the Lamb."

Revelation 7:9-10

Chapter 7

The Sum of All Revelations

14 He will bring glory to me by taking from what is mine and making it known to you. 15 All that belongs to the Father is mine. That is why I said the Spirit will take from what is mine and make it known to you.

John 16:14-15

The Holy Spirit thus far has led me in a discovery of truth, revealing Christ in me, the Hope of Glory, and taking of what is Christ's and showing me the gift Jesus gave to me. I am stunned at its unfolding.

Seasons and the Timing of the Lord

1 There is a time for everything, and a season for every activity under heaven: 2 a time to be born and a time to die, a time to plant and a time to uproot, 3 a time to kill and a time to heal, a time to tear down and a time to build, 4 a time to weep and a time to laugh, a time to mourn and a time to dance, 5 a time to scatter stones and a time to gather them, a time to embrace and a time to refrain, 6 a time to search and a time to give up, a time to keep and a time to throw away, 7 a time to tear and a time to mend, a time to be silent and a time to speak,

Ecclesiastes 3:1-7

As I ponder on the writing and unfolding of this revelation, I am very aware of the Timing of the Lord and the seasons associated with this work. This has been a time and a season for planting and uprooting, a time of mourning and a time of dancing, a time of embrace and a time of refrain, a time of searching and a time to give up, a time of keeping and a time of throwing away, a time of tearing and a time of mending, a time of silence and a time to finally speak. There has also been a time of weeping and intercession and a time of giving birth to the treasure of the Man Child, according to Revelation 12.

I am also keenly aware of the seasons, not according to modern day seasons, but according to the seasons of the Lord as manifested in his appointed seasons and times in the writing of this book. The original unfolding of this revelation occurred during the Feast of Tabernacles in October 2004.

The retelling of the Heavenly Worship Room in Chapter One came during the Feast of Tabernacles in October 2008, and I was able to go back into the room to see it as I first saw it in October 2004. The rest of the revelations came during the Feast of Tabernacles in October 2009 when I began to finish what I had started in this book, a year earlier. The chapter on the Feast of Tabernacles came to its full illumination during the Festival of Lights, as I began to research and write about this Festival. This book and its predecessor has been hidden I believe because the time of Esther is upon us. Incidentally, this manuscript was finally submitted the week of Purim, the festival observing Esther's courage and faithfulness and her people's deliverance.

The vision the Lord gave to the prophetic intercessor of the emptied room in 2004 (though the room was fully furnished and not yet emptied), was accompanied with the vision of the Book of Esther, this corresponds to the festival of Purim. The Lord called me by three names in June of 2000, the first name given to me was Esther. The first Bride Song, of which our ministry derives its name Bride Song Ministries, came in December 2000, "A Lady and Her King." Whenever there is a spirit of Haman on the loose, one whose sole agenda is to destroy the people of God, God will always raise up an Esther or the spirit of Esther within many to destroy the works of this enemy and deliver His people. It is for such a time as this, that Esther was raised up to the heights of the palace, though salvation could come from another, the privilege was given to this woman. I feel that rise within me as I write this portion of the book.

As I survey the Revelation of the Heavenly Worship Room, I stand amazed. The Lord told me that the full understanding of the work to which He called me, now 10 years ago as of this writing, would be fully revealed in the unfolding of the second book, and He is true to His Word. In the full disclosure of the Feast of Tabernacles, I am awed by the spiritual sanctity which undergirds this prophetic room, and renewed in its purpose. In light of the revelation of the Feast of Tabernacles and its relation to the Worship Room, there are fresh insights and a greater purpose emerges.

First of all, the pattern by which the Heavenly Worship Room was constructed has Glory inherent in its design as well as prophetic undertones, of things past, as well as of things to come.

> [11] *"In that day I will restore David's fallen tent. I will repair its broken places, restore its ruins, and build it as it used to be,*
> *Amos 9:11 NIV*

> [11] *In that day will I raise up the tabernacle of David that is fallen, and close up the breaches thereof; and I will raise up his ruins, and I will build it as in the days of old:*
> *Amos 9:11 KJV*

I acknowledge the Revelator and the Creator of this prophetic work, the Lord Himself who said that He would rebuild the Tabernacle of David. It is far beyond my own ability to ever conceive, build, or construct anything of this magnitude, let alone according to fulfillment of scripture in its meaning, revelation, and understanding of its true purpose, or the timing of its resurrection in light of the backdrop of the darkness of the emerging world stage. Everything God does has purpose in His Creation.

His purpose in rebuilding the Tabernacle of David, as has been given to me in its understanding, is to prepare a priesthood, which would again minister directly to Him, and to usher His Glory back into the earth. This is not according to a new modern, contemporary way, but according to His Word which stands outside of time and is inserted in the earth in His perfect timing. His purpose is to prepare and consecrate a Priesthood, and to prepare a Prophetic Sound that when released will usher the Glory back into its residence. This purpose does not stand outside or apart from His finished work upon the Cross, with the death of His Precious Son Jesus. It is fulfilled and only fully realized through the Way made upon the cross, the Way that bridged the gap of separation between the Father and His Creation, and the Holy Way made into the previously forbidden place, the Holy of Holies.

The inherent design is based upon aspects of three tabernacles already given to man, the Tabernacle of Moses, the Tabernacle of David, and the New Testament Tabernacle of Jesus Christ. The Lord said He would rebuild, restore and raise up the fallen tent of David, the Tabernacle of David, as it used to be, but also as in the days of old. This pattern of course refers to the ministry of the priesthood before the Ark of Glory, birthed through David, as well as to the original Tabernacle given to Moses, when he first established the Priesthood ministry. This also refers to the Priesthood and Kingship ministry of the High Priest Melchizedek, predating Moses' establishment of the Levitical priesthood, which also predates time and is eternally established by God Most High. This eternal priesthood is ultimately fulfilled through Jesus Christ who stands eternally as our Mediator and High Priest.

> *¹ Therefore, holy brothers, who share in the heavenly calling, fix your thoughts on Jesus, the apostle and high priest whom we confess. ² He was faithful to the one who appointed him, just as Moses was faithful in all God's house. ³ Jesus has been found worthy of greater honor than Moses, just as the builder of a house has greater honor than the house itself. ⁴ For every house is built by someone, but God is the builder of everything.⁵ Moses was faithful as a servant in all God's house, testifying to what would be said in the future. ⁶ But Christ is faithful as a son over God's house. And we are his house, if we hold on to our courage and the hope of which we boast.*
> *Hebrews 3:1-6*

This is a ministry up close and personal, an encounter and an expression where God and man may meet face to face, the Ultimate Fellowship and Communion.

> *²⁰ Behold, I stand at the door, and knock: if any man hear my voice, and open the door, I will come in to him, and will sup with him, and he with me. ²¹ To him that*

overcometh will I grant to sit with me in my throne, even as I also overcame, and am set down with my Father in his throne.

Revelation 3:20-21 KJV

It can only find its full expression through Jesus Christ, as He is the Way, the Truth, and the Life and the only way to the Father (John 14:6). His body was the veil that was rent in two to part the veil of separation into this Most Holy Place, the Throne Room of God, the Temple of God in Isaiah 6, the Holy of Holies. His All Sufficient, All Covering, and All Sustaining Powerful Blood allows the worshipper to approach in full confidence without the threat of death (Heb.4:16).

The Place where the Ark of the Covenant, the Ark of the Testimony, and the Ark of Glory are fully expressed is the place of the Mercy Seat, where the One sits eternally at the Right Hand of the Father, Jesus Christ Himself.

20 Which he wrought in Christ, when he raised him from the dead, and set him at his own right hand in the heavenly places,

Ephesians 1:20 KJV

6 And hath raised us up together, and made us sit together in heavenly places in Christ Jesus:

Ephesians 2:6 KJV

Our place seated with Him in Heavenly places is firmly secured and allows us access to this place of Glory. In the Worship Room, the Throne is visually represented with the Throne Valance with a veil of translucence before it, though parted in the middle, where the worshipper must press through, as well as the white pillars that frame it. This is not a casual encounter but a Holy approach with a reverence and the Fear of the Lord. The representation of the worshipping Cherubim depicts the Angels who worship and cover Him who sits upon the Throne, the Heavenly worship that surrounds Him day and night, and the angelic accompaniment of worship with us on earth as it is in Heaven. I believe the sounds of angelic worship will accompany the sound of this priesthood, the Bride as she releases her sound in this place of Heaven.

The physical attributes of this room represent the tabernacles of previous days, as in the tent like feel of cloth draping and flowing from the ceiling. The flowing cloth also represents the Romance of the Bride and the King in His Private Chambers, this Holy place of encounter with the Romancer of Heaven, Our Bridegroom and Our King.

The walls are also layered with paint that resembles the Glory (gold) and the Blood (crimson). In previous tabernacles, the animal skin formed the outer walls, representing the sacrificial blood spilled to allow access into the Holy Place. The Blood is represented on the walls as the sacrifice of the One who made our approach to Him accessible. The Golden walls or Glory remind the worshipper that this is not just an earthly dwelling place, but resembles the Glories of Heaven we enter as we worship here. They are His Surroundings, and represent the Majestic Temple of Heaven, which is the Throne Room of Heaven where He is eternally seated.

There is a door to enter this room, where the worshipper gains access.

> *7 Ask, and it shall be given you; seek, and ye shall find; knock, and it shall be opened unto you: 8 For every one that asketh receiveth; and he that seeketh findeth; and to him that knocketh it shall be opened.*
>
> *Matthew 7:7-8 KJV*

> *7 "To the angel of the church in Philadelphia write: These are the words of him who is holy and true, who holds the key of David. What he opens no one can shut, and what he shuts no one can open. 8 I know your deeds. See, I have placed before you an open door that no one can shut. I know that you have little strength, yet you have kept my word and have not denied my name.*
>
> *Revelation 3:7-8*

> *1 After this I looked, and, behold, a door was opened in heaven: and the first voice which I heard was as it were of a trumpet talking with me; which said, Come up hither, and I will shew thee things which must be hereafter.*
>
> *Revelation 4:1 KJV*

This Key of David is in the hands of our Lord and Savior Jesus Christ, who not only possesses the Key of David which unlocks this priesthood ministry again in the earth, but also unlocks the door of the Throne of David, the Throne Jesus is forever seated at His Father's Right Hand, the seat of His Eternal Kingdom. I believe the Key of David also unlocks the only closed door in scripture, the East Gate where the Glory shall once again reenter, the King of Glory shall enter the Temple and the Throne of His Kingdom and the Time of His Reign.

There is another door which enters the platform. This is where the priesthood emerges from the Holy Place and the Audience of One to minister from the Glory to the people. This is a door of transportation into the Heavenly Realm. There is a stairway which represents the angels ascending and descending and where the worshipper ascends into the Higher realms of worship and of Heaven.

The actual teachings of the Room come from the Three Tabernacles represented. The first teaching or station of worship comes from the Tabernacle of Moses, the Bronze (Golden) Laver.

> [12] *"Bring Aaron and his sons to the entrance to the Tent of Meeting and wash them with water.* [13] *Then dress Aaron in the sacred garments, anoint him and consecrate him so he may serve me as priest.* [14] *Bring his sons and dress them in tunics.* [15] *Anoint them just as you anointed their father, so they may serve me as priests. Their anointing will be to a priesthood that will continue for all generations to come."*
>
> *Exodus 40:12-15*

> [7] *And thou shalt set the laver between the tent of the congregation and the altar, and shalt put water therein.* [9] *And thou shalt take the anointing oil, and anoint the tabernacle, and all that is therein, and shalt hallow it, and all the vessels thereof: and it shall be holy.* [11] *And thou shalt anoint the laver and his foot, and sanctify it.* [12] *And thou shalt bring Aaron and his sons unto the door of the tabernacle of the congregation, and wash them with water.* [13] *And thou shalt put upon Aaron the holy*

> *garments, and anoint him, and sanctify him; that he may minister unto me in the priest's office. 14 And thou shalt bring his sons, and clothe them with coats: 15 And thou shalt anoint them, as thou didst anoint their father, that they may minister unto me in the priest's office: for their anointing shall surely be an everlasting priesthood throughout their generations.*
>
> *Exodus 40:7,9,11-15 KJV*

This is a place of consecration God intended for the Priesthood throughout the generations, an eternal ordinance, and an anointing for all those who are in the priest's office, not by man's traditions, but this priestly mantle given by God. This is also the washing of water by the Word, representing where the remnants of the world are washed away and the priest worshipper enters sanctification.

> *25 Husbands, love your wives, even as Christ also loved the church, and gave himself for it; 26 That he might sanctify and cleanse it with the washing of water by the word, 27 That he might present it to himself a glorious church, not having spot, or wrinkle, or any such thing; but that it should be holy and without blemish.*
>
> *Ephesians 5:25-27 KJV*

This room is also a place of transformation as the ways and worries of the world are washed away and the Mind of Christ is singularly focused on things above.

> *2 Do not conform any longer to the pattern of this world, but be transformed by the renewing of your mind. Then you will be able to test and approve what God's will is — his good, pleasing and perfect will.*
>
> *Romans 12:2*

As the Lord brings His Priesthood out of the world where they were dispersed, He must cleanse the world from them, and remove the worldly pattern in sanctification and consecration unto their purpose, the ministry to the Lord Himself and in His House.

The second teaching or worship station of this room is the mirror, which represents not only Moses, who met with God face to face, as a friend, but also Melchizedek who met up close and personally with Abraham. But it is most perfectly demonstrated through the heart of a man who was after God's own heart, David who longed to see the Beauty of the Lord in His Sanctuary. It was David who established the priesthood that ministered directly to the Lord in the Glory and Presence of the Ark in this secret place of His Tabernacle.

This mirror also represents Jesus for as He is so are we in the world.

> *15 But just as he who called you is holy, so be holy in all you do; 16 for it is written: "Be holy, because I am holy."*
> *1 Peter 1:15-16*

> *12 Now we see but a poor reflection as in a mirror; then we shall see face to face. Now I know in part; then I shall know fully, even as I am fully known.*
> *1 Corinthians 13:12*

> *18 But we all, with open face beholding as in a glass the glory of the Lord, are changed into the same image from glory to glory, even as by the Spirit of the Lord.*
> *2 Corinthians 3:18 KJV*

We are being transformed into the very image of the One we are beholding, the image of the Son, and we are being changed from glory to glory, ***every time we peer into Him!*** Everything Jesus said and did was a pattern of revival during his days of ministry, where whole cities and regions flocked to the Glory of the great Miracle Worker, the Great Healer, the Great Teacher, the Great Savior. This mirror also represents Jesus' ultimate purpose which was to reveal His Father back to His Children.

> *7 If you really knew me, you would know my Father as well. From now on, you do know him and have seen him."*
> *9 Jesus answered: "Don't you know me, Philip, even after I have been among you such a long time? Anyone who has seen me has seen the Father. How can you say, 'Show us the Father'? 10 Don't you believe that I am in the Father,*

and that the Father is in me? The words I say to you are not just my own. Rather, it is the Father, living in me, who is doing his work. ¹¹ Believe me when I say that I am in the Father and the Father is in me; or at least believe on the evidence of the miracles themselves.

John 14:7, 9-11

Jesus is the express image of the Father and He came to show us the Father and to reveal His Will which is to seek out worshippers who will worship Him in spirit and in truth.

²³ Yet a time is coming and has now come when the true worshipers will worship the Father in spirit and truth, for they are the kind of worshipers the Father seeks. ²⁴ God is spirit, and his worshipers must worship in spirit and in truth."

John 4:23-24

As we peer into the image of the Son, who is the express image of the Father, we see our Father who is coming to inspect the fruit of the Vine He planted in the earth, fully matured sons and daughters in the full image of His Son. All that Jesus is, we are as well, and we are transformed and become the mirrored reflection of His Glory. As Moses radiated the Glory of God after spending 40 days alone with Him in His Glory, so we will radiate His Glory in our countenance as we spend time with Him in His Glory. Where Moses' radiant and Glorious face faded with time and was concealed with a veil, the Lord's Glory upon us will intensify and shine to the darkness surrounding us, but with a radiance that will not fade, nor be hidden behind a veil.

This mirror with soft flowing fabric also represents the Romance of the Bride and the King, as she readies and prepares herself to be presented before her King. She begins to see herself as the Bride of a Holy King, and the Queen in the Land, designated with all authority given her by her King. And she begins to conduct herself in this manner of authority in a regal manner. Do you remember the word for tabernacle in Chapter 2 was 5521 cukkah or sookkaw, the feminine version of 5520 soke, and also in Matthew 17:4 of Chapter 4, the word 4632 skeuos, which figuratively refers to the wife as contributing to the usefulness of the husband? I believe it was always His intention to tabernacle with her and to continue to conduct His Kingdom business through His Authority given to His Bride, His Wife, the Queen, as exemplified through the life and reign of Queen Esther and His Church.

Not only is this a place for the Prophet, but also a place for the Priest and the King to come forth. After all David, who was a prophet, priest, and King, was the predecessor of who we are in Christ. We are a Royal Priesthood prophesying the Glorious Return of the King of Kings!

The final teaching of this room is the final threshold into this Holy Place, signified by the Table where the Wine Goblet and the Bread are displayed. This wine glass, represents the cup of suffering, the spilled blood of our Lord Jesus Christ and the Wine of the New Covenant, and entrance into His Kingdom.

> [48] *I am the bread of life.* [49] *Your forefathers ate the manna in the desert, yet they died.* [50] *But here is the bread that comes down from heaven, which a man may eat and not die.* [51] *I am the living bread that came down from Heaven. If anyone eats of this bread, he will live forever. This bread is my flesh, which I will give for the life of the world."* [52] *Then the Jews began to argue sharply among themselves, "How can this man give us his flesh to eat?"* [53] *Jesus said to them, "I tell you the truth, unless you eat the flesh of the Son of Man and drink his blood, you have no life in you.* [54] *Whoever eats my flesh and drinks my blood has eternal life, and I will raise him up at the last day.* [55] *For my flesh is real food and my blood is real drink.* [56] *Whoever eats my flesh and drinks my blood remains in me, and I in him.* [57] *Just as the living Father sent me and I live because of the Father, so the one who feeds on me will live because of me.* [58] *This is the bread that came down from heaven. Your forefathers ate manna and died, but he who feeds on this bread will live forever."*
>
> John 6:48-58

This is Jesus' lasting ordinance He gave to His Church to observe in remembrance of Him. He is the Bread of Life, the torn flesh which parted the veil of separation and made entrance into the Holy of Holies forever. The final threshold is not only representing the sacrifice of the One, but the death and sacrifice of the follower, to drink of the cup of sufferings, to allow the Glory and the Life of Christ to manifest fully.

> *17 Now if we are children, then we are heirs —heirs of God and co-heirs with Christ, if indeed we share in his sufferings in order that we may also share in his glory.*
> *18 I consider that our present sufferings are not worth comparing with the glory that will be revealed in us.*
>
> *Romans 8:17-18*

> *10 I want to know Christ and the power of his resurrection and the fellowship of sharing in his sufferings, becoming like him in his death,*
>
> *Philippians 3:10*

Flesh always dies in the Presence of the Glory, and the worshipper must also die to the flesh to enter His glory and inseparable Holiness. This is the True Feast of Tabernacles, the true feast of this room, to feast upon His Word which is the Bread and to drink of His Blood which is the New Wine, within a new wineskin which can contain His Glory and the Fullness of the Life of Christ without bursting. Can you imagine the Glory of this emerging Priesthood, prepared in this secret place of transcending Glory, this Royal Priesthood releasing the Heavenly Sound that ushers the Glory, the King of Glory into His Kingdom? *Selah*

This room is also a place where the breech is fully repaired, the place of intercession where the Priesthood stands before the Lord. As David's priesthood ministered and interceded for 33 years, every year of the life Jesus Christ lived on the earth, how much more is this place of intercession which makes way in the Glory for the Return of the King? *Selah*

When Jesus came before, he came on a humble donkey, his way paved by palm branches, an earthly material. Not so the second time. This priesthood will pave the way with Glory (of Heaven) for the return of the Almighty King, not upon a donkey, but a majestic white stallion, in a manner worthy of the King of Kings, the King of Heaven!

This place of intercession also finds its true expression in the revelation of the Feast of Tabernacles. As the priesthood encircled the altar, in the same manner as in the Battle of Jericho in which the walls of the city fell down, so this priesthood intercedes for the nations to come to the full knowledge of the King and His Kingdom. The Feast of Tabernacles is also known as the Feast of Gentiles where all the nations shall observe this Feast and worship the Lord.

> 16 Then the survivors from all the nations that have attacked Jerusalem will go up year after year to worship the King, the LORD Almighty, and to celebrate the Feast of Tabernacles. 17 If any of the peoples of the earth do not go up to Jerusalem to worship the King, the LORD Almighty, they will have no rain.
>
> Zechariah 14:16-17

The other aspects of the Feast of Tabernacles that are revealed in their truest light is that it was established by Moses as a reminder of the booths or tabernacles that housed the Israelites during their wilderness days. As part of the Feast, they were to live in these booths for seven days. How does this tie in to the Tabernacles of Moses, David, and Jesus Christ? Remember it was in these booths that the Israelites learned how to worship God.

> 10 And all the people saw the cloudy pillar stand at the tabernacle door: and all the people rose up and worshipped, every man in his tent door. 11 And the LORD spake unto Moses face to face, as a man speaketh unto his friend. And he turned again into the camp: but his servant Joshua, the son of Nun, a young man, departed not out of the tabernacle.
>
> Exodus 33:10-11 KJV

> 10 Whenever the people saw the pillar of cloud standing at the entrance to the tent, they all stood and worshiped, each at the entrance to his tent. 11 The LORD would speak to Moses face to face, as a man speaks with his friend. Then Moses would return to the camp, but his young aide Joshua son of Nun did not leave the tent.
>
> Exodus 33:10-11

As their leader Moses met face to face with the Glory of the One and Only, the Israelites learned true worship, and worshipped at the entrance of their booths or at their "tent door." As these leaders worship in the Glory unto the Lord Himself, they will then lead in true worship and the people will then learn how to truly worship the Lord in His Glory.

As this priesthood stands firm the ground as in Joshua 3, the whole assembly shall cross over from First Day and Second Day worship into Third Day worship, accompanied with Glory and with Heaven. We will cross over into the eternal worship we see in the Book of Revelations and elsewhere in scripture. This is the true worship that the Father seeks that will fill the earth as it also fills all of Heaven. I believe this is why I saw many of these rooms go up in this nation and many other nations, just like booths in the Feast of Tabernacles. These booths or rooms are where the sound of Third Day worship is birthed and prepared, where the Habitation of Glory resides ("Lovely are your dwelling places!"), where sounds of earth are infused with the sounds of Heaven. A place where the worshipper is immersed in the glory and being transformed into the Image of the Son! I cannot fully express the Glory and the Worship that will come, it cannot be contained in this book or in any limited expression!

As in the days of David, he delegated scribes to record and pen these glorious verses called Psalms, which they also used in their worship. I believe in these places, new Psalms have yet to be written and recorded. Part of the purpose of these rooms is to record all that takes place in these Heavenly encounters, scripture as it comes alive, songs of Heaven, Sounds of Heaven, Angelic visitation, visions and revelations of Heaven. The encounters alone will be all consuming and life transforming. His Glory is upon me now as I, as a scribe, pen the experience that will come to the worshipper in this place. In my heart I believe it is too wonderful for me, and I can barely contain what I am experiencing in anticipation of its true calling. I am being drawn into His Presence and answer the calling of His Invitation. *Selah* Will you? *Selah* As my journey through this revelation has come to its conclusion, I stumbled on something very significant. I was writing the bibliography of this book, and through further research, discovered that the author the Lord led me to concerning the Feast of Tabernacles was Alfred Edersheim. I was stunned in my discovery. I did not know anything about him, I was just drawn to his writing. I discovered that his insights mirrored and confirmed my writing and confirmed the very aspects of the room. What I did not know was that he was a Jewish scholar who was raised as a Jew and lived from 1825–1889. Edersheim was educated in the Talmud and Torah, and converted to Christianity in the mid-1840s. He later became the pre-eminent Christian-Jewish scholar of the 19th century. His writings written 130 years previously confirmed the prophetic nature of the Heavenly Worship Room. I am stunned, yet I am reminded that Jesus is the same, yesterday, today and tomorrow, and He confirms His Word, sometimes before it is even performed!

The Court of Women

There are several more aspects of the Feast of Tabernacles to which I want to bring understanding. This Feast was a joyous celebration, as there is fullness of Joy in His Presence. As part of the ceremony, they descended into the Court of Women, where it is noted that great preparations were made. I remember when I was preparing this room, I was very meticulous to the vision I was given, so as to precisely bring forth this work according to the pattern I had received. Some may have felt it was religious in its approach, though I did not. I did not want to misrepresent or veer off the blueprint, as I really had no idea in its fullness of what I was doing. Not until the writing of the last chapter was it fully revealed to me what I was doing and the significance of every detail of this work.

During the preparation of this room, there were several impressions that I understood in what I was doing. First of all, it was in the time approaching Christmas, and I was very aware of the fact that when Jesus came the first time, no room was made for him, and that I was preparing a room for him. I was also reminded that a wife prepares her living room in her own taste and style to make a place of rest for her husband when he returns from his hard day of labor. This is a place where he is comfortable and at peace in his surroundings, where his wife comes and sits beside him as he unwinds, while his children climb up into his lap. I was very mindful at the time that this is what I was doing, preparing a place where the Lord was comfortable in His Surroundings, a place that resembled Heaven, where His Wife could come and sit with him and his children could climb up in their Papa's lap; His Living Room, His Habitation, His Residence, His Dwelling Place with man. This perfectly corresponds to the great preparations made within the Court of Women, only fully revealed to me a chapter ago.

In the Court of Women were four golden candelabras, each with four golden bowls, four ladders and four priestly youths, with golden pitchers containing oil. Every one of these aspects are represented within the room, from the golden candelabras to the golden bowl, the golden pitcher, the oil, and the stairway (ladder). The candelabra, of which I found two of the same design, one smaller than the other, had a raised candle in the middle, representing the Lord, the Light of the World, and four lower candles surrounding the one, which represents us as the Church fulfilling the Great Commission to go into all of the world, in every direction, North, South, East and West, sharing the Gospel, making disciples of men and nations. This also brings us back to Zechariah 14:16.

There were other items, such as pillows and chairs, in the room to merely provide comfort for the worshipper, as they lose themselves in hours of worship in His Presence and in His Glory.

I am also fully persuaded that the purpose of the room is revealed in two very important aspects of the Feast of Tabernacles, the Pouring out of Water, and the Illumination.

The Pouring out of Water

I did not realize the pitcher was symbolic of the gathering of the water from the Pool of Siloam. The manner that they gathered the water was similar to when the Israelites gathered the manna daily in the wilderness. A double portion was gathered the previous day to be reserved for the Sabbath. Similarly, the water was gathered for the Sabbath and reserved in the Temple in the golden pitcher, and for the Sabbath, the water already gathered in the golden vessel was poured out from within the Temple, thus represented by the golden pitcher in the room.

I believe this aspect represents the Healing that takes place here, as the Blind Man was healed by Jesus in the Pool of Siloam, during this same Feast. We are healed in His Presence, and we are healed as we worship Him in this glorious place of Heaven. The golden laver was to contain water within this room. The Pouring out of wine and water together represents the Blood and Water that poured out of Jesus' side; the Pouring of the wine of the New Covenant of Grace, and the Pouring out of Living Water. The same Living Water exemplified in Ezekiel's Temple when it was poured out, went into the sea of lost humanity, and everything that was dead would live again. By the way, there is supposed to be such a River of Living Water flowing out from the altar within the Temple and within the Church that brings life to all who are flooded by it!

The Wonder of Hurricane Harvey

One of the most remarkable wonders was the flooding caused by Hurricane Harvey that not only hit Texas, on August 25th, 2017 but literally camped over the Region of Houston, Texas unexplainably for over three days, with over 19 trillion gallons of water in Texas alone. Amidst the devastation, the despair, and the massive cleanup, I was reminded of Ezekiel's Temple and the River that flowed from it. I not only remembered the flooding of water that filled the homes, the streets and the waters that were too high to cross, but I saw the Glory filling the streets, the homes, the families and everywhere the River flowed, Life would bring everything that was dead back to life, the lost sea of humanity to life!

The River From the Temple

¹ The man brought me back to the entrance to the temple, and I saw water coming out from under the threshold of the temple toward the east (for the temple faced east). The water was coming down from under the south side of the temple, south of the altar. ² He then brought me out through the north gate and led me around the outside to the outer gate facing east, and the water was trickling from the south side. ³ As the man went eastward with a measuring line in his hand, he measured off a thousand cubits and then led me through water that was ankle-deep. ⁴ He measured off another thousand cubits and led me through water that was knee-deep. He measured off another thousand and led me through water that was up to the waist. ⁵ He measured off another thousand, but now it was a river that I could not cross, because the water had risen and was deep enough to swim in—a river that no one could cross. [6] He asked me, "Son of man, do you see this?" Then he led me back to the bank of the river. [7] When I arrived there, I saw a great number of trees on each side of the river. [8] He said to me, "This water flows toward the eastern region and goes down into the Arabah, where it enters the Dead Sea. When it empties into the sea, the salty water there becomes fresh. [9] Swarms of living creatures will live wherever the river flows. There will be large numbers of fish, because this water flows there and makes the salt water fresh; so where the river flows everything will live. [12] Fruit trees of all kinds will grow on both banks of the river. Their leaves will not wither, nor will their fruit fail. Every month they will bear fruit, because the water from the sanctuary flows to them. Their fruit will serve for food and their leaves for healing."

Ezekiel 47 1-9, 12 NIV

The Illumination

The illumination of the Temple was similar to the Pouring out of Water which was associated with the Shekinah Glory that filled Solomon's Temple. This was brought forth in the room through the lights that lined the ceiling and the soft glow within the room from the floor lamp and sconces as well as the lit candelabras. The illumination was also to be portrayed through the artwork that would be displayed in this room, an expression to invoke worship unto the Lord. The artist who was commissioned to paint the picture under the Throne Valance was taught by the Lord in how to bring forth the Glory and Illumination through his painting. I was very excited in anticipation of seeing this painting go into the room and to see the Illuminated Glory captured on canvas, but it was not finished in time. But most of all, the illumination came from the reflection of the light upon the walls that enabled the walls to dance with the Glory. I believe these rooms, these booths will so radiate the Glory, that they will look like lighthouses to the darkening storms of the world surrounding them, as well as to the Church as a whole.

The greatest significance of this work will be a sign to the Jewish nation, through their understanding and performing the customs and ceremonies of the Feast of Tabernacles, they will see that Jesus truly is the Light of the world. When the Jewish nation sees the Glory, the same Glory they recognize from their History, not only in Moses' Tabernacle but residing in Solomon's Temple, I believe they will recognize the Source of Glory, Jesus Christ as their true Messiah, and His Glory will radiate from His Church.

Miracles of Resurrection and Restoration

As of the publishing of The Heavenly Worship Room, in its second edition, many miracles have taken place. The first miracle was the added facet of the Key of David as an actual higher tuning from A440Hz to A444Hz. I have already had several worship services where all the instruments tuned up to 444hz and it has been immediately felt in the atmosphere, the ease of prophetic flow, and the unity of the spirit in worship.

The second miracle was the Lord's Sovereign Hand restoring the Heavenly Worship Room in its function. The final function of the room which I did not talk much about, was recording the Worship Music that inhabited that room. My friend Gary McClatchy who was my original drummer during that time, and had also done some recording for me, returned to the place, and the pastor gave him the Heavenly Worship Room to record any of his worship projects. While we are awaiting the publishing of this book, we are beginning to record in the Heavenly Worship Room, which has remained dormant for over 13 years now.

The next miracle was finding the original artist I had commissioned for the painting of the Lord in it's original construction in October 2004. We had lost touch, and I had over the years looked for him and could not find him anywhere. I got off the phone with my publisher, and thought about giving him one more try, and to my utter astonishment, I found him and his artwork. I am so excited to feature that original picture of The Glory of The Lord in this book. Many incredible miracles have taken place just in the last week concerning the Heavenly Worship Room.

The most profound revelation unfolded just this morning, August 11, 2017. The Lord had spoken clearly to my broken heart in 2005, that he would restore David's fallen tent, He would also restore

Raelynn's fallen tent. I held onto that promise to this very day. About September of last year, I and my husband Paul Parkin and our four children began to help repair and restore my father and mother's lake house in Livingston, Texas. We just felt compelled to do it no matter what it took, and we worked hard, especially my husband Paul and our sons, rebuilding front porches, restoring front and back decks, and lots of boxes and paint! It was an overwhelming job, which we finished mid July 2017. The understanding came this morning as I heard those words again, "I will restore David's fallen tent, I will restore Raelynn's fallen tent. My natural father's name is David Semones, and as we worked hard to restore his fallen tent, the Lord was working to restore mine! Selah.

Not only that, but the Lord had reminded me that King David had it in his heart to build the House for the Lord, but as he was a man of war, the task would fall to his son Solomon, who would build it in a time of Peace. However, David provided the gold and silver and treasures to furnish the Temple his son Solomon would build.

He provided a large amount of iron to make nails for the doors of the gateways and for the fittings, and more bronze than could be weighed. He also provided more cedar logs than could be counted, for the Sidonians and Tyrians had brought large numbers of them to David. David said, "My son Solomon is young and inexperienced, and the house to be built for the Lord should be of great magnificence and fame and splendor in the sight of all the nations. Therefore I will make preparations for it." So David made extensive preparations before his death. "I have taken great pains to provide for the temple of the Lord a hundred thousand talents of gold, a million talents of silver, quantities of bronze and iron too great to be weighed, and wood and stone. And you may add to them.

1 Chronicles 22:3-5, 14

When all the work King Solomon had done for the temple of the Lord was finished, he brought in the things his father David had dedicated—the silver and gold and the furnishings—and he placed them in the treasuries of the Lord's temple.

1 Kings 7:51

David made provision for his son Solomon to complete the task of building the Temple. My natural father is David, and I am David's daughter, and the promise of provision was reassuring as I set out to complete my God given mandate and mission.

The final piece of my identity was revealed to me in a simple Sunday School class on a November morning. In the final hours of my childbirth, my father was waiting in the hall with my grandparents during my delivery. Back then, fathers were not allowed in the delivery room during childbirth. To my grandmother's utter dismay, my father pronounced that he was going to name me "Jedidiah Gunch!" He finally settled on my name Raelynn and everyone was happy, but it was always a funny reminder, my entire life, of who I almost became! So during this recent class, our teacher began to talk about Jedidiah. No one really knew who this guy was, especially me. Jedidiah was the second name or Blessing name of the Lord for Solomon, conferred by God through the prophet Nathan during Solomon's infancy. Found in 2 Samuel 12:25, Jedidiah is a token of divine favor, meaning "Beloved by Jehovah or Beloved of Yah or Friend of the Lord." King Solomon, also known as King Jedidiah, was responsible for the building of the House of the Lord, though it is unknown by which name he used during his reign. Some scholars believe Jedidiah was his Throne name, while Solomon was given by his father David, meaning "peaceable." The names David and Jedidiah are related in that they mean Beloved. Though my father David did not realize the significance of this event, he was literally prophesying my identity and my calling at my birth! All I can say is "Glory to God!"

The last miracle was the Resurrection and Restoration of all that seemed to be lost. I had dismantled the Heavenly Worship Room on Friday before Thanksgiving, November 19, 2004. I only visited the room a couple of times in the following years. One of my original worship team members, Rev. Jerry Stitt, who is in his late 80's, approached me at a mutual worship friend's funeral in order to tell me, that the Lord had instructed him to play his saxophone in the Room, even in the dark, thus keeping the lights on, which he faithfully and periodically did over the years. On August 11, 2017, I reentered the Heavenly Worship Room, for the first time in over 13 years, for the purpose of recording the worship.

I met my amazing worship friend, co-laborer and original drummer in the room, Gary McClatchy, and we caught up, took some pictures, and reminisced about past glorious experiences together in worship. We then prayed, had the Lord's communion, and recorded our first worship CD of The Heavenly Worship Room Worship series. And it was a glorious beginning and a promise of many more glorious encounters to come. Overwhelming gratitude, satisfaction, and overflowing joy flooded my spirit as we rejoiced in the Goodness and Faithfulness of our God! Praise his Holy Name! All of the missing pieces have been reunited for one beautiful Tapestry of his Glory! And there will be many more to come! Selah

Some final developments during the republishing of The Heavenly Worship Room came into view as we continued to record the worship in The Chronicles of Worship. We began to see more of the fulfillment and the fruition of what had begun more than 13 years ago. In The Trumpets CD, we blew the shofar and the trumpets exactly two weeks before Rosh HaShanah, as well as during this festival, the Feast of Trumpets. We then recorded the Generations CD, and to my astonishment, there were elements specific to the Court of Women, the tradition of the Temple celebration of the first day of the Feast of Tabernacles. An element of the Tabernacle of David was the legacy of the fathers training up the sons to prophesy on their instruments in the Ministry before the ark of Glory. In the Court of Women, there were four young priests represented. In our recording of the Generations CD, there were also four young priests represented, two were my natural born sons, Zachary and Michael, whom I had trained for over ten years to worship in the Glory Realm. There were two of my spiritual sons, whom I had also trained in the Glory, Robert Steele on Trumpet who worshiped with me for over 10 years, and Gary McClatchy, who had worshiped with me in the Glory 15 years earlier. It was truly profound to bring these generational priests together to worship in the Glory Realm again.

Another interesting aspect of the project, was that we crossed over into the Jewish Head of the Year, Rosh Hashanah, Year 5778. It is profound that the name of the year and its prophetic meaning is The Open Door, which is the front cover of my book The Heavenly Worship Room. The actual walls of the room are its background and there is a doorknob with a key in the keyhole, with glory radiating from it. In essence, when you open the front cover, The Door, it is as if you are entering the Heavenly Worship Room. How significant is this in the Timing of the Lord! It was amazing as we began to worship in the room, the previous year 5777 was the Clashing of the Swords, and there was significant spiritual warfare at the beginning of the worship project, so we assembled an army of Intercessors to join us as we recorded. As we crossed over the New Year, there was a greater peace and rest and ease of the flow of recording.

The most profound aspect of all, was that we were able to celebrate our very first Feast of Tabernacles in The Heavenly Worship Room, Thursday thru Saturday, October 5th, 6th, and 7th. We were celebrating the Feast of Tabernacles in our Booth, the Heavenly Worship Room! I began to look at other images of The Feast of Tabernacles, and they looked exactly as the Original Heavenly Worship Room had looked in its creation! I did not know in October 2004, that I was building a Booth for the Feast of Tabernacles! I am still awestruck! We celebrated the Feast of Tabernacles with daily communion with the Lord, and we worshiped the Lord with great joy, The Season of our Joy! We recorded two separate elements of the Chronicles of Worship Project, the Intimate Place and the Highest Prasie CDs, both profound aspects of the Celebration of the Feast of Tabernacles. We had not specifically planned this, they just happened to be the days our musicians could join us! But the Lord knew exactly what He wanted to hear and what we brought forth in our recordings!

Thirteen years ago, when I was asked to dismantle The Heavenly Worship Room, the Lord spoke to my heart, that the "baby" was snatched up to Heaven, according to Revelation 12, but it would return a fully grown man!

...The dragon stood in front of the woman who was about to give birth, so that it might devour her child the moment he was born. ⁵ She gave birth to a son, a male child, who

"will rule all the nations with an iron scepter." And her child was snatched up to God and to his throne. ⁶ The woman fled into the wilderness to a place prepared for her by God, where she might be taken care of for 1,260 days.
Revelation 12:4b-6 NIV

I had always believed for the Resurrection and the Restoration, but I was truly amazed at the full maturity of the Heavenly Worship Room, and all of its amazing aspects of Divine Restoration! It has been truly a "Season of our Joy" to me in our Return to the Heavenly Worship Room! I believe it is The Lord's Heart to not just document the origin of The Heavenly Worship Room, but to display the Glorious Hand of the Lord to deliver us into the Fulfillment, the Resurrection, and the Restoration of it and to see the Signs, the Miracles and the Wonders of what He has accomplished! All I can say is Glory to God for who He is and what He has demonstrated for us!

Famine in the Land

There was once a famine in the land, a famine for the Word of the Lord during the prophetic silence of 400 years between the Old and New Testament. Jesus broke that silence as the Word made flesh and fed the starving people the Living Word from God, so much that all that He said and did could not be contained in many books, according to John's closing statements (John 21:25). The Church and the World have been in a famine of the Glory, since the mid 300's A.D., when the lights of the Church nearly went out and we entered the Dark Ages. (Constantine declared Christianity to be the official religion of the state, and the Glory of the Church was intermingled in pagan temples of idolatry and mixed with pagan customs). God always kept his Flame burning through single candles throughout History that was never fully extinguished.

But we have not seen the Glory in the Church, as in the early days where Great Glory was birthed and flourished through great persecution. The Glory of this Latter House shall be greater than of the former, not only of Solomon's Temple, but greater than the Glory that was witnessed in the early Church. The Lord Himself shall fully satisfy the hunger of His Church with His Glory that shall overwhelm and flow out of His

Church. This Glory shall be even greater than that which He left in the earth, for He is not coming for less than what He started with. He is coming for the full fruition of what was originally sown in the earth. He was the seed that died and abided alone but shall result in the Greatest days of Harvest the earth has ever seen!

Conclusion

As we near the end of this living epistle, we are brought full circle to the Master Builder of His House. He chose his first precious living stone, the Cornerstone, and from that stone, he quarried many new stones to build a Living House made of Living Stones.

> *4 As you come to him, the living Stone— rejected by men but chosen by God and precious to him— 5 you also, like living stones, are being built into a spiritual house to be a holy priesthood, offering spiritual sacrifices acceptable to God through Jesus Christ.*
>
> *1 Peter 2:4-5*

In Revelation 21, the angel shows John the Bride, the wife of the Lamb and what she looks like, a Holy City coming from Heaven with 12 gates which are the 12 tribes of Israel (whom we entered to find our Messiah and Savior, Jesus Christ), and 12 foundations which are the 12 apostles of the Lord's Church. In this new city, there is no Temple in the city, for the Lord Himself is its Temple, and the Light of His Glory gives light to the world. Its purpose, besides its gorgeous display of the Glory of the Almighty God, is to give His Light to the nations. This is the ultimate purpose of the Bride, to shine His Glory to the nations.

> *9 One of the seven angels who had the seven bowls full of the seven last plagues came and said to me, "Come, I will show you the bride, the wife of the Lamb." 10 And he carried me away in the Spirit to a mountain great and high, and showed me the Holy City, Jerusalem, coming down out of heaven from God. 11 It shone with the glory of God, and its brilliance was like that of a very precious jewel, like a jasper, clear as crystal. 12 It had a great, high wall with twelve gates, and with twelve angels at the gates. On the gates were written the names of the twelve tribes of Israel. 13 There were three gates on the east, three on the north, three on the south and three on the west.*

¹⁴ The wall of the city had twelve foundations, and on them were the names of the twelve apostles of the Lamb. ²² I did not see a temple in the city, because the Lord God Almighty and the Lamb are its temple. ²³ The city does not need the sun or the moon to shine on it, for the glory of God gives it light, and the Lamb is its lamp. ²⁴ The nations will walk by its light, and the kings of the earth will bring their splendor into it. ²⁵ On no day will its gates ever be shut, for there will be no night there. ²⁶ The glory and honor of the nations will be brought into it. ²⁷ Nothing impure will ever enter it, nor will anyone who does what is shameful or deceitful, but only those whose names are written in the Lamb's book of life.

Revelation 21:9-14, 22-27

I was once asked whether I could lead worship without the Heavenly Worship Room. What they did not understand as part of that equation was that the room was in me! I could no more divorce myself than I could abolish the Most Holy Place, the indwelling of the Holy Spirit, and the secret place within me where I meet with the Lord and I enter into His Rest, meeting with the indwelling Glory of God! When I worship, as well as when I lead worship, I open the door into this Most Holy Place and usher the Body into this inner sanctum, the Private Chambers of the Lord.

⁹ As Moses went into the tent, the pillar of cloud would come down and stay at the entrance, while the LORD spoke with Moses. ¹⁰ Whenever the people saw the pillar of cloud standing at the entrance to the tent, they all stood and worshiped, each at the entrance to his tent. ¹¹ The LORD would speak to Moses face to face, as a man speaks with his friend. Then Moses would return to the camp, but his young aide Joshua son of Nun did not leave the tent.

Exodus 33:9-11

Jesus once said that there were many rooms in His Father's House.

² In my Father's house are many rooms; if it were not so, I would have told you. I am going there to prepare a place for you. ³ And if I go and prepare a place for you, I will come back and take you to be with me that you also may be where I am.

John 14:2-3

I am a room in My Father's House, a House He is building with living stones, and this room is within me. Jesus said that where He was, there I may be also, and that I would have my being in that place with Him. I am a Temple of God which Temple is Holy. Oh Lord that you would prepare me to be a Holy Sanctuary for You!

The Lord said that He would repair the breech within David's Tabernacle. This breech is the place where His Priesthood stood before the Glory. It was a place of intercession, a place where they could boldly approach His Throne of Grace, both in David's Tabernacle and now in Jesus' New Testament Tabernacle. As He draws back His Priesthood from the world where they have been dispersed, He must take the world out of these musicians, consecrate them, set them apart, and bring them back to the true ministry of the House of the Lord, the ministry of the One and Only, as in the commission of the Sons of Zadok in Ezekiel's time.

¹⁵ "'But the priests, who are Levites and descendants of Zadok and who faithfully carried out the duties of my sanctuary when the Israelites went astray from me, are to come near to minister before me; they are to stand before me to offer sacrifices of fat and blood, declares the Sovereign LORD. ¹⁶ They alone are to enter my sanctuary; they alone are to come near my table to minister before me and perform my service.' "

Ezekiel 44:15-16

This Room is as much a teaching room as it is a room of separation unto the Lord, a room of preparing the Priesthood, a place of intercession, and a room of ministry unto the One and Only, the Lord. It is a place where the Habitation of Glory can indwell, take up its residence, and pour forth from the Temple once again to flood a city, immersing the nation and the Church with His Glory. This room is also a place where the Sounds of Heaven are heard, where the Sounds of Heaven envelope the worshipper, and the Sounds of the Glory and the Great Revival are conceived, nurtured, and finally birthed into the earth. It is a place where the realm of earth is left, and the worshipper accesses the realms of Heaven, literally a place of transportation.

In Heaven, the elders adore and worship the Lord together with the angels of Heaven. The worship of elders and angels are enmeshed and the Glory that is sung about is then poured out in demonstration as to who He is, saturating every part of Heaven. We sing and believe and even recite the Lord's Prayer, "...Thy Kingdom come, Thy Will be done, on earth as it is in Heaven." I believe this to be a place where that can truly be fulfilled. This room is a place where saints and angels cover the Throne, as in Heaven, so also in the earth, and the sounds that come forth in this place are of Heaven's origins, Heaven's Sounds, and Heaven's design being poured forth from broken earthen vessels.

But as the Glory of God and the Holiness of God are inseparable, so the worshipper must die to the flesh, as flesh always dies in the Presence of the Glory, (as in Uzzah's case). Jesus prepared the way into this Holy Place with the rending of His own flesh, which was exemplified with the rending of the curtain of separation in the Temple upon His Death, and the pouring out of His Blood which covers us in this Holy Place. He made a way for these worshippers to have access to the very Throne Room of God from a life of rending the flesh, a pouring out of themselves as a drink offering unto the Lord, under the Cover of His Precious Son's Blood that was shed on our behalf. They may approach without the penalty of death as the Sons of Zadok, the Priesthood that ministered before the Ark of Glory, and may also be sustained in the Glory as that Glory is ushered into its residence.

The priests of Solomon's Temple were unable to minister because of the magnificent Glory that was ushered in. Moses also was unable to minister as the Glory was ushered into the Tabernacle.

> [13]The trumpeters and singers joined in unison, as with one voice, to give praise and thanks to the LORD. Accompanied by trumpets, cymbals and other instruments, they raised their voices in praise to the

LORD and sang: "He is good; his love endures forever. Then the temple of the LORD was filled with a cloud, ¹⁴ and the priests could not perform their service because of the cloud, for the glory of the LORD filled the temple of God.

2 Chronicles 5:13-14

³³ Then Moses set up the courtyard around the tabernacle and altar and put up the curtain at the entrance to the courtyard. And so Moses finished the work. The Glory of the LORD ³⁴ Then the cloud covered the Tent of Meeting, and the glory of the LORD filled the tabernacle. ³⁵ Moses could not enter the Tent of Meeting because the cloud had settled upon it, and the glory of the LORD filled the tabernacle.

Exodus 40:33-35

I believe because of our position with Christ where we are seated in Heavenly places with him (Ephesians 2:6), and because He as our High Priest of this eternal Priesthood of Melchizedek, has gone before us and covers us, we may minister in that Glory and be sustained by his Keeping Power, clothed in His Robes of Righteousness, as a Holy Nation and a Royal Priesthood (1 Peter 2:9).

When we finally enter into this ministry of the priesthood, this will be the beginning of the fulfillment of Amos 9:11, where God says He will rebuild the Tabernacle of David as well as rebuilding the priesthood ministry within this Tabernacle.

¹¹In that day will I raise up the tabernacle of David that is fallen, and close up the breaches thereof; and I will raise up his ruins, and I will build it as in the days of old:

Amos 9:11 KJV

¹¹ "In that day I will restore David's fallen tent. I will repair its broken places, restore its ruins, and build it as it used to be,

Amos 9:11 NIV

I believe this also to be the beginning of the fulfillment of Hosea 6:2, entering the third day where we may live in His Presence.

² After two days he will revive us; on the third day he will restore us, that we may live in his presence.

Hosea 6:2

This becomes a life, and a lifestyle, where you will lose your life, the one you knew before, in the Glory, and you will find the Life of Christ in this Glorious Place of His Presence. You will be transformed from Glory to Glory as you peer into the image of the Son in worship, in this place of His Presence, His Glory, where He is seated above the Mercy Seat in His Tabernacle, His Dwelling Place with men.

¹⁸ But we all, with open face beholding as in a glass the glory of the Lord, are changed into the same image from glory to glory, even as by the Spirit of the Lord.

2 Corinthians 3:18

¹² Now we see but a poor reflection as in a mirror; then we shall see face to face. Now I know in part; then I shall know fully, even as I am fully known.

1 Corinthians 13:12

I believe this to also be the beginning of the fulfillment of Haggai 2:6-9, where the Glory of the Latter House shall be greater than of the Former House, Solomon's Temple. I believe we are already seeing verses 6-8 being fulfilled before our very eyes!

⁶ For thus saith the LORD of hosts; Yet once, it is a little while, and I will shake the heavens, and the earth, and the sea, and the dry land; ⁷ And I will shake all nations, and the desire of all nations shall come: and I will fill this house with glory, saith the LORD of hosts. ⁸ The silver is mine, and the gold is mine, saith the LORD of hosts. ⁹ The glory of this latter house shall be greater than of the former, saith the LORD of hosts: and in this place will I give peace, saith the LORD of hosts.

Haggai 2:6-9 KJV

In the former House there was only one Temple, one Holy of Holies, one Mercy Seat, and one residence for the Glory of God. In the vision I saw in October 2004, I saw many of these rooms emerge, and I believe to be the greater Glory, in that there are more places of His Habitation, more places of this priesthood ministry, more places of the Tabernacle of David being built in the earth. There are more places where worshippers are being changed from Glory to Glory, more places of intercession where the priesthood positionally stands before the Lord. There are more places where the Sounds of Heaven are birthed, are prepared, and invade the earth; where the Sounds of Heaven are released to usher in the Glory back into the Church and in the earth.

I believe this to also be the fulfillment of the mighty Joel's Army, where 3rd day worshippers are assembled and go as a mighty army and also before the mighty army of the Lord.

> ² *a day of darkness and gloom, a day of clouds and blackness. Like dawn spreading across the mountains a large and mighty army comes, such as never was of old nor ever will be in ages to come.* ³ *Before them fire devours, behind them a flame blazes. Before them the land is like the garden of Eden, behind them, a desert waste — nothing escapes them.* ⁴ *They have the appearance of horses; they gallop along like cavalry.* ⁵ *With a noise like that of chariots they leap over the mountaintops, like a crackling fire consuming stubble, like a mighty army drawn up for battle.* ⁶ *At the sight of them, nations are in anguish; every face turns pale.* ⁷ *They charge like warriors; they scale walls like soldiers. They all march in line, not swerving from their course.* ⁸ *They do not jostle each other; each marches straight ahead. They plunge through defenses without breaking ranks.* ⁹ *They rush upon the city; they run along the wall. They climb into the houses; like thieves they enter through the windows.*
>
> *Joel 2:2-9*

Jesus declared that we would do even greater things than those He did while He was with us. I believe this was not only the work of salvation which would go to the ends of the earth, but as Jesus was in one place, so Jesus through many vessels can do more and be in more places.

> ¹¹ *Believe me when I say that I am in the Father and the Father is in me; or at least believe on the evidence of the*

miracles themselves. ¹² *I tell you the truth, anyone who has faith in me will do what I have been doing. He will do even greater things than these, because I am going to the Father.* ¹³ *And I will do whatever you ask in my name, so that the Son may bring glory to the Father.*

John 14:11-13

Jesus, the Hope of Glory, can be poured from many arks, His Habitation can be housed through many dwelling places, and His Glory as manifested through many can fill the whole earth, for He did say that the whole earth was filled with His Glory.

¹⁴ *For the earth will be filled with the knowledge of the glory of the LORD, as the waters cover the sea.*

Habakkuk 2:14

It is not enough to just give birth to many babies. The Father is looking for the fullness of the Image of His Son through many. The Gardener, who is the Father, is coming to inspect His Fruit, birthed through the seed that abided alone, the death of His Son. He is not coming for small sprigs of leaves, but He is coming for full ripe fruit! He is coming for the fully manifested sons and daughters, fully manifesting the Image and Glory of His Son, the Mighty Oaks of Righteousness, the Fully Matured Church, looking, walking, speaking in authority in the same magnitude as His Son.

¹ *"I am the true vine, and my Father is the gardener.* ² *He cuts off every branch in me that bears no fruit, while every branch that does bear fruit he prunes so that it will be even more fruitful.* ³ *You are already clean because of the word I have spoken to you.* ⁴ *Remain in me, and I will remain in you. No branch can bear fruit by itself; it must remain in the vine. Neither can you bear fruit unless you remain in me.* ⁵ *"I am the vine; you are the branches. If a man remains in me and I in him, he will bear much fruit; apart from me you can do nothing.* ⁶ *If anyone does not remain in me, he is like a branch that is thrown away and withers; such branches are picked up, thrown into the fire and burned.* ⁷ *If you remain in me and my words remain*

in you, ask whatever you wish, and it will be given you.
8 This is to my Father's glory, that you bear much fruit,
showing yourselves to be my disciples.

John 15:1-8

For this reason, the Church must make the journey from first day (salvation) to second day (manifesting the Holy Spirit and His gifts) and not stop there until they reach the pinnacle of the third day, where His Presence is fully manifested through the sons of God. We are witness to the earth's groaning as in the pains of childbirth for the manifested sons and daughters to come forth in the earth, the return of the Son in His Fullness, as He once walked in the earth, now through many.

21 that the creation itself will be liberated from its bondage
to decay and brought into the glorious freedom of the
children of God. 22 We know that the whole creation has
been groaning as in the pains of childbirth right up to the
present time.

Romans 8:21-22

This priesthood of worshippers must go into the river as when Joshua and the Israelites crossed the Jordan River, not one, but many, and stand in the middle of that river. We must stand firm that ground until the whole Church has crossed over to the other side, from wilderness wanderers to full possessors of the Promised Land, as exemplified by our High Priest, Jesus Christ.

2 After three days the officers went throughout the camp,
3 giving orders to the people: "When you see the ark of the
covenant of the LORD your God, and the priests, who
are Levites, carrying it, you are to move out from your
positions and follow it. 4 Then you will know which way
to go, since you have never been this way before 5 Joshua
told the people, "Consecrate yourselves, for tomorrow the
LORD will do amazing things among you." 6 Joshua said
to the priests, "Take up the ark of the covenant and pass on
ahead of the people." So they took it up and went ahead of
them. 8 Tell the priests who carry the ark of the covenant:
'When you reach the edge of the Jordan's waters, go and

stand in the river.' "[17] *The priests who carried the ark of the covenant of the LORD stood firm on dry ground in the middle of the Jordan, while all Israel passed by until the whole nation had completed the crossing on dry ground.*

Joshua 2-6,8, 17

[10] *Now the priests who carried the ark remained standing in the middle of the Jordan until everything the LORD had commanded Joshua was done by the people, just as Moses had directed Joshua. The people hurried over,* [11] *and as soon as all of them had crossed, the ark of the LORD and the priests came to the other side while the people watched.*

Joshua 4:10-11

When the arks of His Glory come together and the cover is removed, what kind of Glory will be spilled out of these treasured vessels? What Sound of Heaven can be poured forth from these instruments of worship? Is this not truly, "Thy Kingdom come, Thy Will be done, on earth as it is in Heaven?" Where the bridge was made complete by the sacrifice of One spotless Lamb, Jesus Christ, the earth looks like Heaven in these places of His Glory. Where worship is of Heaven, in that place of Heaven, there is no sickness or disease (there is no sickness in Heaven!). Isn't this why Jesus came, to bridge the gap where we would no longer be separated from God, and all that is from Him? A place where we could walk with God in the cool of the day as Adam did, where the Father could be reunited with His children and His Creation, this living way made through His Son.

Can the earth contain this kind of Glory, or will it have to release them, as Jesus ascended before, is this possibly the reason for the rapture? The earth cannot contain the Glory, but it returns from where it came, Heaven and the Father! After all, Jesus was glorified in the earth, and many witnessed His Glory before He ascended into Heaven.

The King is coming for His Bride, for she has made herself ready and is prepared as the wise virgin bride full of the Oil of the Holy Spirit. Do you want to know how close the King is in His Coming for the Bride? Look to the Bride! She is a mere reflection of His Glory, a mirrored image of the Son. The closer the King comes in his approach, the more Glorious and Radiant is the Bride. Watch the Bride! As in marriage ceremonies even today, everyone stands up and watches the Bride as she is ushered in to meet her Bridegroom. How radiant and how beautiful is she, as everyone sighs in wonder at the Beauty of the Bride!

> 9 Then the angel said to me, "Write: 'Blessed are those who are invited to the wedding supper of the Lamb!'" "And he added, "These are the true words of God."
> Revelation 19:9

All who are invited to witness the marriage supper of the Lamb shall rejoice in the coming together of the Bride and the Bridegroom. And all of Heaven applauds as the Father gives away the Bride to be presented to the King of all Kings! Read the words of this psalm the Lord gave me on August 25, 2001, as they are coming into the fullness of their time.

I'm wooing you as a lover
I long for your embrace
I long for your kiss of worship Intimate
moments with you
I'll take you to the deep
The deep places of My Heart
There I'll teach you to swim
Have no fear, I won't let go.

Places you have never been
Places you can't ever go
Without me leading you there.
I call out to My Beloved
Will you come out and play?
Will you come learn of me
And partake of what I've freely given?

I will adorn you as a Bride
With jewels and Pearls of honor
I will lavish you as My Queen
With treasures untold.

Be still and let me dress you
In My Royal Robes of Righteousness.

Then you may come to me
And ask of me anything
And I'll give it to you.
Ask me anything and I'll give it to you.
The destruction of your enemy
His head on a silver platter,
Up to half of the Kingdom

You have pleased me.
Ask of me, it is yours.
Ask of me, I am yours.

For all these things you already have in me.
All these things I am to you.
Ask and it shall be given unto you.
For as you have humbled yourself as
My Bride and My Queen
My grace in great measure is coming to you.
Grace that gives you strength,
Grace that is my Power.
For you shall stand in places you have never known.
My Grace is there for you.
It is your sufficiency.
Let go of who you think you are.
Hold on to who you are in me.
For that is your place of strength, it's hidden in me.

As you rest in the depths of my Heart,
I have arisen as Your Champion.
I am mighty on your behalf to save you.
As you stay in that place of rest in me,
No fear can touch you there.

For I'm your First Husband, and I will give you rest.
I will fight your battles, only rest in me.
I will extinguish your enemies, only rest in me.

I am your Pillar of Cloud by day,
To guide you through the wilderness,
To shield and protect you
From the scorching sun of your trials.
Find joy in me, for I am covering you.

I am your pillar of fire that stands
Between your enemy and you.
He cannot even see you through me.

I am taking you across mighty waters
But I am taking you on dry land.
Your foot shall not slip or even get wet.

For I am taking you to the Promise.
The Promise I have made you
You will not see that enemy anymore
For I have destroyed him before your eyes.

Do not forget where I have taken you.
For you need to remember for the battles ahead.
But I have not called you to fight them on your own.

Behold the Mighty Arm of the Lord
That goes before you.
My armies of angels are discharged
To fight on your behalf.
As you walk in faith, they are in step with you.
If you hold back, and do not go forward,
They will stop and wait for you.

You are my generals
And they are awaiting my commands.
I am sending my commands through your mouthpiece.
According to My Authority in you,
For we are marching towards the greatest battle
My church has ever known.
Take heart, I have overcome the world
And I shall overcome the world through you.
Every place your foot touches

Shall be possession of the land taken back in my name.

The enemy may appear to be giants,
But they are quaking in fear
FOR THEY HAVE NEVER SEEN THE BRIDEGROOM ARISE
WITH SUCH POWER IN THE BRIDE
AS SHE STEPS FORWARD.
LOOK, it is HE arising in you
That makes them quake in their boots.

For He is stepping on the property through His Beloved
The enemy is running and leaving all the loot behind.
The Manifested Bride shall take back
What the enemy has stolen from the people of God.
And she leaves a wake of destruction in her path.
All power and authority shall be reestablished to her,
Who represents the Bridegroom, the King.

And He shall come back to receive her unto Himself,
The Glorious Bride adorned as a Queen.
Walking in the full glory of her King.
For as He was in the world, so shall she be.

She has cleaned her garments
And made them spotless and without wrinkle.
Her face radiates the glory of her King
And becomes brighter as He approaches.
She is walking in the power and authority
That He left with her.
She is holy unto Him.
She is wholly His, set apart for only His Touch.

She is more magnificent and more beautiful
Than He ever imagined.
The King is enthralled with her beauty.
His breath catches in His Throat as He approaches her.
His love beats passionately in His Heart for her.
And her heart can think of nothing else
But the consummation of His Love,

And the completion of her desire for Him.

The Holy Spirit takes her by the hand
And He delivers her into the hand of her King
As they approach the Wedding Supper of the Lamb.

Written by the Holy Spirit of Promise August 25, 2001

Bibliography

1. Strong, James. The New Strong's Exhaustive Concordance of the Bible. Nashville: Thomas Nelson Publishers, 1990.

2. Vine, W.E. Vine's Concise Dictionary of the Bible. Nashville: Thomas Nelson Publishers, 2005.

3. Edersheim, Alfred. (October 1997). "The Temple – It's Ministry and Services" Retrieved October 28, 2009 from the website: http://www.Philologos.org

4. Pardue, Steve. (January 19, 2010). "Jesus is Our Passover Lamb" Retrieved October 28, 2009 from the website: http://www.cynet.com/jesus/PROPHECY/Cr ucifixion.htm

5. Fairchild, Mary. (January 19, 2010). "Feast of Pentecost" Retrieved October 28, 2009 from the website: http://christianity.about.com/od/biblefeast sandholidays/p/pentecostfeast.htm

6. Tyrrell, Michael S. The Sound of Healing: Unveiling the Phenomena of Wholetones. Brandon, South Dakota: Barton Publishing, 2015. Print.

7. LaRive, Dwayne, "The Glory of the Lord." Published with permission by Artist. Facebook.com/LaRive Artworks

About the Author

Dr. Raelynn Parkin and her husband Paul founded their ministry, Bride Song Ministries in 2007. She was ordained in 2003 as a worship leader and minister of the gospel. Her ministry centers around the Bride Song to the King, and leading the Body of Christ into the Holy of Holies where she ministers from. In 2007, she authored her first book, "Lessons from One Worship Leader to Another." The second updated edition is called "Unlocking Worship Entering His Presence." In February 2008, she completed her first teaching conference called "Unlocking Worship," in which she taught the lessons of her book in 8 sessions. The message of her book is to properly prepare the worshipping priesthood in how to carry the Glory and how to enter into the Holy of Holies through worship. This priesthood will establish an atmosphere of Glory in the church, which sets an environment for signs, wonders, and miracles to come into the mainstream church of America today. Through her teaching series, she has prophesied the Latter House of Glory that is coming into the Church. Her vision is to fully equip and to ignite the worshippers through teaching and impartation to fulfill their calling of ushering the Glory back into the Church through worship. She and her husband Paul currently host "The Lord's Bridal Company" which is an intimate soaking service that draws the Body into the Holy of Holies through worship in their home monthly.

Dr. Raelynn Parkin recently received her Doctorate of Divinity from CICA University in October 2016, and is also recognized as a U.N. Ambassador At Large through CICA University as well as a Chaplain. She currently teaches and leads worship in conferences, worship events and other speaking engagements in and around Houston.

Other Resources by Bride Song Ministries

Books and Teaching Resources

Unlocking Worship Entering His Presence $15.95

This book explores worship ministry according to the Word of God, exposes the strategies of the enemy that hinder the Glory, establishes precepts of the worshiping priesthood and ultimately declares what must be present to see the glory of God return back to the Church, especially the American Church.

Conversations Bride Songs and Psalms to the King $15.95

Compilation of Bridal poetry received from the Lord including the Bride Songs and other intimate conversations with the Lord.

Unlocking Worship Teaching Series
8 sessions $30.00

This teaching series builds upon the original principles of the book, "Lessons from One Worship Leader to Another," (now in its second edition, the updated version Unlocking Worship Entering His Presence) with fresh revelation, anointing and application above and beyond what is contained in the book.

Music CDs

Chronicles of Worship 8 CD Series $80.00

Chronicles of Worship is the music of The Heavenly Worship Room, which demonstrates the facets of the Room as well as brings the music of Heaven to earth.

The Lord's Bridal Company Vol. 1 CD $10.00

A Live Worship Night Experience soaking in an
atmosphere of Heaven.

The Lord's Bridal Company Vol. 2 CD $15.00

A live recording featuring 11 musicians
Prophesying the intimate songs from Out of the
Secret Place and the Bride Songs Studio projects.

Out of the Secret Place CD $15.00

Worship from the Secret Place

Bride Songs A Lady and Her King CD $15.00

A treasury of Songs of romance from the Bride to the King.

Arise My Church Arise Live CD $15.00

The Live recording from the Arise My Church Arise
Summer Houston Tour featuring 11 prophetic artists.

To order these resources, go to
www.bridesongministries.org
Or www.raelynnparkin.com
Or www.chroniclesofworship.org
Or email your request to bridesong.raelynn@gmail.com
Or via mail, write your check to Bride Song Ministries, to include $5 shipping/handling, and mail to:
Bride Song Ministries,
18311 Trace Forest Drive,
Spring, Texas 77379.

Printed in the USA
CPSIA information can be obtained
at www.ICGtesting.com
LVHW060014111023
760671LV00015B/434/J